William Harrison Lambert

**Memory Gems**

Graded Selections in Prose and Verse

William Harrison Lambert

**Memory Gems**

*Graded Selections in Prose and Verse*

ISBN/EAN: 9783337372200

Printed in Europe, USA, Canada, Australia, Japan

Cover: Foto ©Thomas Meinert / pixelio.de

More available books at **www.hansebooks.com**

# MEMORY GEMS:

## GRADED SELECTIONS IN PROSE AND VERSE,

### FOR THE USE OF SCHOOLS.

BY

**W. H. LAMBERT,**

SUPERINTENDENT OF SCHOOLS, MALDEN, MASS.

---

We should lay up in our minds a store of goodly thoughts in well-wrought words, which should be a living treasure of knowledge, always with us, and from which, at various times, and amidst all the shifting of circumstances, we might be sure of drawing some comfort, guidance, and sympathy. — ARTHUR HELPS.

---

BOSTON:
PUBLISHED BY GINN, HEATH, & CO.
1883.

*The thanks of the editor are due to* MESSRS. HOUGHTON, MIFFLIN & CO., *for the generous permission to use passages from their copyrighted authors.*

# PREFACE.

THE value of committing to memory in childhood choice passages of prose and verse cannot be overrated. Although the practice as a school exercise is of late introduction among us, yet it has long been insisted on in the programmes of schools in England, and especially on the continent of Europe. It was made much of by the early writers on education, and it is now recognized by the best teachers everywhere as an essential part of school training. As a means of moral culture, it is of inestimable importance. The elevated and noble sentiments the selections embody refine the manners, exalt the feelings, and stimulate the moral energies of the child. He who when a boy stores his mind with the best precepts for the guidance of life, cannot go far astray when a man. A recitation of "memory gems" should be made each morning a part of the opening exercises of the school. What better preparation for the day's work can the teacher make, than by bathing, as it were, the minds of his pupils in the living fountains of thought which have issued from the noblest souls.

The teacher should see to it that the selections are not committed mechanically. It is not simply the words that are to be put in the memory — it is the thought that is to be made felt. The passages to be committed should be explained, and their meaning enforced. With younger children, especially, it is well for the teacher first to repeat the exercise, thus by example inculcating the proper tones and inflections. To derive from these exercises the benefit which they contemplate, the passages committed should often be reproduced. The pupil should not only be able to *say* the selection, but he should repeat it so often that it becomes inwoven with the very fibre of his mind.

This book contains three hundred and forty-six "gems," selected from more than one hundred and fifty authors, and embraces a wide range of thought and sentiment. The selections have been arranged in three groups, for primary, intermediate, and advanced classes. A closer gradation seems to the editor impracticable.

The book has been prepared with a firm conviction of the importance of the practice which it is designed to encourage, and is offered in the hope that teachers may be assisted by it in making such selections as are most worthy to be treasured in the minds of those under their charge.

MALDEN, December 22, 1883.

# INDEX OF AUTHORS.

Abbey, Henry, 90.
Addison, Joseph, 91.
Alger, Horatio, 50.
Alger, W. R., 95.

Bacon, Francis, 135.
Bailey, Philip J., 84, 86, 142.
Banks, G. L., 86.
Barbauld, Mrs. Letitia, 131.
Barry, Michael J., 142.
Benjamin, Park, 76.
Berkeley, Bishop George, 83.
Blake, William, 35.
Bonar, H., 92.
Bossuet, 125.
Browning, Robert, 100.
Browning, Elizabeth Barrett, 58.
Bryant, William C., 106, 128, 148.
Burke, Edmund, 104.
Burns, Robert, 87, 120, 136.
Butler, Samuel, 95.
Butts, Mrs. M. F., 9.
Byrd, William, 93.
Byron, Lord, 111, 113, 136, 144.

Campbell, Thomas, 94.
Cary, Alice, 63, 75.
Cary, Phœbe, 22.
Carlyle, Thomas, 104, 116.

Chesterfield, Lord, 116.
Child, Lydia Maria, 30.
Cicero, 132.
Clark, Luella, 24, 41.
Clough, Arthur Hugh, 142, 144.
Cook, Eliza, 53.
Coleridge, S. T., 33, 77.
Colesworthy, M. D. C., 65, 105.
Confucius, 143.
Congreve, William, 131.
Cornwall, Barry, 124.
Cotton, Nathaniel, 149.
Cowper, William, 95, 117, 122.
Cranch, C. P., 91.

Dickens, Charles, 130.
Dodge, Mary Mapes, 48, 49.
Doddridge, Philip, 141.
Dolcken, H. W., 18, 23.
Douglass, Marian, 23.
Drake, Joseph Rodman, 119.
Dwight, Timothy, 118.
Dwight, J. S., 125.
Dyer, Edward, 109.

Earle, N., 68.
Eliot, George, 150.
Eliot, Henrietta R., 56.
Elliot, Ebenezer, 126.

## INDEX OF AUTHORS.

Emerson, Ralph Waldo, 67, 96, 117, 134, 137, 142.
Epictetus, 131.
Erasmus, 129.

Faber, F. W., 106.
Fairholt, F. W., 53.
Fawcett, Edgar, 49.
Fichte, 136.
Fields, James T., 51, 97.
Fletcher, John, 89.
Follen, Mrs. Eliza, 33.

Garrison, William Lloyd, 99.
Goethe, 122.
Goldsmith, Oliver, 151.
Goodwin, Mrs., 28.
Gough, John B., 122.
Gray, Thomas, 88.

Hale, Mrs., 108.
Hall, Bishop, 103.
Hamilton, Alexander, 117.
Hawkesworth, Mrs., 77.
Heath, C. B., 69.
Herrick, Robert, 87.
Herbert, George, 101.
Hillhouse, James H., 140.
Holland, J. G., 108, 115, 135.
Holmes, O. W., 102.
Houghton, George, 90, 139.
Houghton, Lord, 135.

Ingelow, Jean, 38, 64.

Jefferson, Thomas, 152.
Jewett, Sarah O., 17.
Jones, Sir William, 121.
Jonson, Ben, 133.

Keats, John, 99.
Keble, John, 118.
Kingsley, Charles, 28, 59, 62, 101.

Larcom, Lucy, 20, 66, 127, 140.
Locke, John, 107.
Longfellow, H. W., 42, 61, 74, 79, 94, 95, 98, 113, 115, 120, 129, 131, 144, 149, 150.
Lowell, James Russell, 125, 143.
Lovelace, Richard, 94.
Lytton, Bulwer, 113, 129, 134.

Macdonald, George, 3.
Mackay, Charles, 57.
Massey, Gerald, 116.
Mathews, William, 138.
McCarthy, Dennis Florence, 132.
Milton, John, 105, 147.
Montgomery, James, 91, 137.
Moore, Thomas, 118.

Newman, J. H., 89.

O'Reilly, John Boyle, 90.
Osgood, F. S., 90.
Osgood, H. S., 98.

Pitt, William, 153.
Plautus, 119.
Plutarch, 115.
Pope, Alexander, 105, 129, 134, 141.
Porter, President, 112.
Prescott, Mary M., 39.
Preston, Margaret J., 101.

Reynolds, Bishop, 104.
Rochester, Earl of, 109.

Rogers, Samuel, 145.
Rosetti, Christina G., 100.
Ruskin, John, 133.
Savage, M. J., 96.
Saxe, J. G., 97.
Schiller, 138, 146.
Scott, Sir Walter, 93, 110, 151.
Seneca, 128.
Shakespeare, William, 89, 92, 100, 103, 104, 105, 106, 107, 108, 109, 110, 111, 112, 113, 114, 115, 116, 117, 118, 119, 120, 121, 123, 124, 126, 127, 129, 130, 141, 145, 148, 149.
Shelley, Percy Bysshe, 88.
Southey, Robert, 98.
Stael, Madame de, 137.
Stacy, Joel, 9.
Stodart, M. A., 16.
Story, W. W., 143.

Talfourd, T. N., 147.
Tennyson, Alfred, 7, 72, 83, 84, 110, 114, 123, 130, 135, 139, 141, 143.
Thackeray, William M., 133.
Thomson, James, 99.
Trench, Richard Chevevix, 102.

Ware, Henry, Jr., 126.
Watts, Isaac, 50.
Webster, Daniel, 123.
Whittier, J. G., 55, 111.
Wilcox, Carlos, 84.
Wise, Henry A., 54.
Wordsworth, William, 85, 92, 102, 109, 129, 132, 136, 140.
Wotton, Sir Henry, 112.

Young, Edward, 96, 146.

# PRIMARY CLASSES.

# Selections for Primary Classes.

## THE BABY.

Where did you come from, baby dear?
Out of the everywhere into here.

Where did you get your eyes so blue?
Out of the skies as I came through.

Where did you get that little tear?
I found it waiting when I got here.

What makes your forehead so smooth and high?
A soft hand stroked it as I went by.

What makes your cheek like a warm white rose?
I saw something better than any one knows:

Whence that three-cornered smile of bliss?
Three angels gave me at once a kiss.

Where did you get this pearly ear?
God spoke, and it came out to hear.

Where did you get these arms and hands?
Love made itself into hooks and bands.

Feet, whence did you come, you darling things?
From the same box as the cherubs' wings.

How did they all come to be just you?
God thought of me, and so I grew.

But how did you come to us, you dear?
God thought of you, and so I'm here.

Geo. Macdonald.

## THE CHILD'S WORLD.

Great, wide, beautiful, wonderful world,
With the wonderful water round you curled,
And the wonderful grass upon your breast —
World, you are beautifully drest.

The wonderful air is over me,
And the wonderful wind is shaking the tree;
It walks on the water, and whirls the mills,
And talks to itself on the tops of the hills.

You friendly earth! how far do you go
With the wheat-fields that nod and the rivers that flow,
With cities, and gardens, and cliffs, and isles,
And people upon you for thousands of miles?

Ah! you are so great and I am so small,
I tremble to think of you, world, at all;
And yet, when I said my prayers to-day,
A whisper inside me seemed to say:
You are more than the earth, though you are such a dot;
You can love and think, and the earth cannot.

*Lilliput Lectures.*

## A GOOD NAME.

Children, choose it,
Don't refuse it;
'Tis a precious diadem;
Highly prize it,
Don't despise it;
You will need it when you are men.

Love and cherish,
Keep and nourish;
'Tis more precious far than gold;
Watch and guard it,
Don't discard it;
You will need it when you are old.

## TWO AND ONE.

Two ears and only one mouth have you;
The reason, I think, is clear:
It teaches, my child, that it will not do
To talk about all you hear.

Two eyes and only one mouth have you;
The reason of this must be,
That you should learn that it will not do
To talk about all you see.

Two hands and only one mouth have you,
And it is worth while repeating:
The two are for work you will have to do —
The one is for eating.

## MOTION RECITATION.

This is east, and this way west,
Soon I'll learn to say the rest;
This is high, and this is low,
Only see how much I know.
This is narrow, this is wide,
Something else I know beside.

Down is where my feet you see,
Up is where my head should be;
Here's my nose, and here my eyes;
Don't you think I'm getting wise?
Now my eyes wide open keep,
Shut them when I go to sleep.

Here's my mouth, and here's my chin,
Soon to read I shall begin;
Ears I have as you can see,
Of much use they are to me!
This my right hand is, you see.
This my left, as all agree;
Overhead I raise them high,
Clap! clap! clap! I let them fly.

If a lady in the street,
Or my teacher I should meet,
From my head my cap I take,
And a bow like this I make.
Now I fold my arms up so,
To my seat I softly go.

## LITTLE BIRDIE.

What does little birdie say,
In her nest at peep of day?
"Let me fly," says little birdie,
"Mother, let me fly away."

"Birdie, rest a little longer,
Till the little wings are stronger."
So she rests a little longer,
Then she flies away.

What does little baby say,
In her bed at peep of day?
Baby says, like little birdie,
"Let me rise and fly away."

"Baby, sleep a little longer,
Till the little limbs are stronger.
If she sleeps a little longer,
Baby, too, shall fly away."

ALFRED TENNYSON.

## TWINKLE, TWINKLE, LITTLE STAR.

Twinkle, twinkle, little star!
How I wonder what you are,
Up above the world so high,
Like a diamond in the sky.

When the glorious sun is set,
When the grass with dew is wet,

Then you show your little light,
Twinkle, twinkle all the night.

In the dark-blue sky you keep,
And often through my curtains peep,
For you never shut your eye,
Till the sun is in the sky.

As your bright and tiny spark
Guides the traveller in the dark,
Though I know not what you are,
Twinkle, twinkle, little star!

## THE ANGEL'S LADDER.

"If there were a ladder, mother,
　　Between the earth and sky,
As in the days of the Bible,
　　I would bid you all good-by,
And go through every country,
　　And search from town to town,
Till I had found the ladder,
　　With angels coming down.

"Then I would wait quite softly,
　　Beside the lowest round,
Till the sweetest-looking angel
　　Had stepped upon the ground;
I would pull his dazzling garment,
　　And speak out very plain,
Will you take me, please, to heaven,
　　When you go back again?"

"Ah, darling," said the mother,
  "You need not wander so
To find the golden ladder
  Where angels come and go.
Wherever gentle kindness
  Or pitying love abounds,
There is the wondrous ladder,
  With angels on the rounds."
                                MRS. M. F. BUTTS.

## THE SWEET RED ROSE.

"GOOD-MORROW, little rose-bush,
  Now prythee tell me true:
To be as sweet as a sweet red rose,
  What must a body do?"

"To be as sweet as a sweet red rose,
  A little girl like you
Just grows, and grows, and grows, and grows, —
  And that's what she must do."
                                JOEL STACY.

## BAD "I CAN'T."

"Leave our school-room,
  Bad 'I Can't';
Leave it now forever!
  We will try, and try again,
And listen to you never.

"Leave us, leave us,
    Bad 'I Can't';
You have naughty brothers, —
    'Will,' and 'Shall,' and 'Won't,' and 'Shan't,'
And too many others.

"Good-by, good-by,
    Bad 'I Can't';
Shut the door behind you;
    In this school-room nevermore
Shall our teacher find you."

*Our Little Ones.*

## DON'T FRET.

Don't be in a pet;
You never should fret,
But laugh, and try to be good.
You never should scold;
Do what you are told,
As little ones always should.

## BE CHEERFUL.

Try to be cheerful;
Never be fearful,
Or think that the sky will fall.
Let the sky tumble,
Fear not the rumble,
It never can hurt you at all.

## BE A MAN.

O FIE!
Do not cry,
If you hit your toe;
Say "Oh!"
And let it go.
Be a man
If you can,
And do not cry.

## HASTE IS WASTE.

LIVE and learn;
Do not burn
Your fingers in the fire.
Do not run,
Just for fun,
Your little legs to tire.
Learn to talk,
Learn to walk,
But do not be in haste;
Stub your toes,
Hurt your nose,
And learn that haste is waste.

Do your best, your very best,
    And do it every day,
Little boys and little girls,
    That is the wisest way.

## GOD'S LOVE.

God cares for every little child
    That on this large earth liveth;
He gives them home and food and clothes,
    And more than these God giveth.

He gives them all their loving friends,
    He gives each child its mother;
He gives them all the happiness
    Of loving one another.

He makes the earth all beautiful;
    He makes thine eyes to see;
And touch and hearing, taste and smell,
    He gives them all to thee.

What can a little child give God?
    From his bright Heavens above
The great God smiles and reaches down,
    To take his children's love.

## NEVER PLAY TRUANT.

Listen to me, now,
    My dear little lad:
Never play truant;
    'Tis naughty and bad.

Others will scorn you,
    And point as you pass:
"Look at the boy
    At the foot of his class!"

While you are growing
  Learn all that you can,
Or you will be sorry
  When you are a man.

## THE CHILD AND THE RAIN-DROPS.

PITTER-PATTER, pitter-patter,
  On the window-pane!
Oh, where do you come from,
  You little drops of rain?

Pitter-patter, pitter-patter,
  Is what I hear you say;
Tell me, little rain-drops,
  Is this the way you play?

I sit here at the window;
  I've nothing else to do;
Oh, how I'd like to play
  This rainy day with you!

The little rain-drops cannot speak;
  But, "pitter-patter, pat"
Means, "we play on this side,
  But you must play on that."

## THE GOLDEN RULE.

To do to all men as I would
  That they should do to me,
Will make me kind, and just, and good,
  And so I'll try to be.

## A CHILD'S WISH.

I WISH I were a note
From a sweet bird's throat!
I'd float on forever,
And melt away never!
I would I were a note
From a sweet bird's throat!

But I am what I am!
As content as a lamb.
No new state I'll covet;
For how long should I love it?
No, I'll be what I am, —
As content as a lamb!

## THE BOY WHO NEVER TOLD A LIE.

ONCE there was a little boy,
  With curly hair and pleasant eye —
A boy who always told the truth,
  And never, never told a lie.

And when he trotted off to school,
  The children all about would cry,
"There goes the curly-headed boy —
  The boy that never tells a lie."

And everybody loved him so,
  Because he always told the truth,
That every day, as he grew up,
  'Twas said, "There goes the honest youth."

And when the people that stood near
  Would turn to ask the reason why,
The answer would be always this:
  "Because he never tells a lie."

## GOD'S CARE.

KNOWEST thou how many stars
There are shining in the sky?
Knowest thou how many clouds
Every day go floating by?
God, the Lord, has counted all;
He would miss one, should it fall.

Knowest thou how many babes
Go to little beds at night,
That, without a care or trouble,
Wake up with the morning light?
God, in Heaven, each name can tell,
Knows thee too, and loves thee well.

## HARK! MY CHILDREN!

HARK! hark! O my children, hark!
    When the sky has lost its blue,
What do the stars sing in the dark?
    "We must sparkle, sparkle through."

What do leaves say in the storm,
    Tossed in whispering heaps together?
"We can keep the violets warm,
    Till they wake in fairer weather."

What do happy birdies say,
    Flitting through the gloomy wood?
"We must sing the gloom away —
    Sun or shadow — God is good."

## THE DARLING LITTLE GIRL.

Who's the darling little girl
    Everybody loves to see?
She it is whose sunny face
    Is as sweet as sweet can be.

Who's the darling little girl
    Everybody loves to hear?
She it is whose pleasant voice
    Falls like music on the ear.

Who's the darling little girl
    Everybody loves to know?
She it is whose acts and thoughts
    All are pure as whitest snow.

## ONE THING AT A TIME.

Work while you work,
    Play while you play;
This is the way
    To be cheerful and gay.

All that you do
    Do with your might;
Things done by halves
    Are never done right.

One thing each time,
    And that done well,
Is a very good rule,
    As many can tell.

Moments are useless
   Trifled away;
So work while you work,
   And play while you play.

M. A. STODART.

## DISCONTENT.

DOWN in a field, one day in June,
   The flowers all bloomed together,
Save one, who tried to hide herself,
   And drooped that pleasant weather.

A robin, who had flown too high,
   And felt a little lazy,
Was resting near a buttercup
   Who wished she were a daisy.

For daisies grew so trig and tall!
   She always had a passion
For wearing frills around her neck,
   In just the daisies' fashion.

And buttercups must always be
   The same old tiresome color;
While daisies dress in gold and white,
   Although their gold is duller.

"Dear Robin," said the sad young flower,
   "Perhaps you'd not mind trying
To find a nice white frill for me,
   Some day when you are flying?"

"You silly thing!" the robin said,
  "I think you must be crazy:
I'd rather be my honest self,
  Than any made-up daisy.

"You're nicer in your own bright gown,
  The little children love you;
Be the best buttercup you can,
  And think no flower above you.

"Though swallows leave me out of sight.
  We'd better keep our places;
Perhaps the world would all go wrong
  With one too many daisies.

"Look bravely up into the sky,
  And be content with knowing
That God wished for a buttercup
  Just here, where you are growing."
                              SARAH O. JEWETT.

## PATIENCE.

THE fisher who draws his net too soon,
  Won't have any fish to sell;
The child who shuts up his book too soon,
  Won't learn any lessons well.

For if you would have your learning stay,
  Be patient, don't learn too fast;
The man who travels a mile each day,
  Will get round the world at last.
                              H. W. DOLCKEN.

## STOP, STOP, PRETTY WATER!

"Stop, stop, pretty water!"
　Said Mary, one day,
To a frolicksome brook
　That was running away.

"You run on so fast!
　I wish you would stay;
My boat and my flowers
　You will carry away.

"But I will run after,—
　Mother says that I may,—
For I would know where
　You are running away."

So Mary ran on;
　But I have heard say,
That she never could find
　Where the brook ran away.

## CHILDREN.

Oh, blessed things are children —
　The gifts of heavenly love!
They stand betwixt our worldly hearts
　And better things above.
They link us with the spirit world
　By purity and truth,
And keep our hearts still fresh and young
　With the presence of their youth!

*From "Blackwood."*

## THE SONG OF THE THRUSH.

There's a merry brown thrush sitting up in the tree:
   He's singing to me! he's singing to me!
And what does he say, little girl, little boy?
   "Oh, the world's running over with joy!
      Don't you hear? Don't you see?
      Hush! look! in my tree
   I'm as happy as happy can be!"

And the brown thrush keeps singing, "A nest, do you see,
   And five eggs hid by me in the juniper tree?
Don't meddle, don't touch, little girl, little boy,
   Or the world will lose some of its joy;
      Now I'm glad! now I'm free!
      And I always shall be,
If you never bring sorrow to me."

So the merry brown thrush sings away in the tree,
   To you and to me, to you and to me;
And he sings all the day, little girl, little boy:
   "Oh, the world's running over with joy!
      But long it won't be —
      Don't you know? don't you see?
Unless we are as good as can be!"
Lucy Larcom.

---

If wisdom's ways you wisely seek,
   Five things observe with care:
To whom you speak, of whom you speak,
   And how, and when, and where.

## TIME.

"Sixty seconds make a minute,
　　Sixty minutes make an hour;"
If I were a little linnet,
　　Hopping in her leafy bower,
Then I should not have to sing it:
"Sixty seconds make a minute."

"Twenty-four hours make a day,
　　Seven days will make a week;"
And while we all at marbles play,
　　Or run at cunning "hide and seek,"
Or in the garden gather flowers,
We'll tell the time that make the hours.

In every month the weeks are four,
　　And twelve whole months will make a year;
Now I must say it o'er and o'er,
　　Or else it never will be clear;
So once again I will begin it:
"Sixty seconds make a minute."

## THE WISEST PLAN.

Suppose, my little lady,
　　Your doll should break her head,
Could you make it whole by crying
　　Till your eyes and nose were red?
Then wouldn't it be pleasanter
　　To treat it as a joke,
And say you're glad 'twas dolly's,
　　And not your head that's broke?

Suppose your task, my little man,
    Is very hard to get,
Will it make it any easier
    For you to sit and fret?
Then wouldn't it be wiser,
    Than waiting like a dunce,
To go to work in earnest,
    And learn the thing at once?

Suppose the world doesn't please you,
    Nor the way some people do,
Do you think the whole creation
    Will be altered, just for you?
Then isn't it, my boy or girl,
    The wisest, bravest plan,
Whatever comes, or doesn't come,
    To do the best you can?

PHŒBE CARY.

## KIND WORDS.

KIND words can never die —
    Cherished and blessed;
God knows how deep they lie,
    Stored in the breast.
Like childhood's simple rhymes,
Said o'er a thousand times,
Ay, in all years and climes,
    Distant and near,
Kind words can never die;
Deep in the soul they lie,
    God knows how dear.

## THE SONG OF THE BEE.

Buzz-z-z-z-z — buzz!
This is the song of the bee.
   His legs are of yellow,
   A jolly good fellow,
And yet a great worker is he.

In days that are sunny
He's getting his honey;
In days that are cloudy
   He's getting his wax:
On pinks and on lilies,
And gay daffodillies,
And columbine blossoms
   He levies a tax.

   Buzz-z-z-z-z — buzz!
From morning's first gray light,
Till fading of daylight,
He's singing and toiling
   The summer day through.
Oh! we may get weary
And think work is dreary:
'Tis harder by far
   To have nothing to do.
MARIAN DOUGLAS.

## SPEAK THE TRUTH.

Speak the truth, and speak it ever,
   Cost it what it will;
He who hides the wrong he did,
   Does the wrong thing still.
H. W. DOLCKEN.

## POLITENESS.

Good boys and girls should never say
  "I will!" and "give me these!"
Oh, no; that never is the way,
  But, "Mother, if you please."

And "If you please," to sister Ann,
  Good boys to say are ready;
And "Yes, sir," to a gentleman,
  And "Yes, ma'am," to a lady.

---

## DO YOUR DUTY!

Do your duty! little man,
  That is the way;
There's some duty in the plan
  Of every day.
Every day has some new task
  For your hand;
Do it bravely, — that's the way
  Life grows grand.

"Do your duty!" say the stars,
  That so bright,
Through the midnight's dusky bars,
  Drop their light.
"Do your duty!" says the sun,
  High in heaven;
To dutiful, when tasks are done,
  Crowns are given —

Crowns of power and crowns of fame —
    Crowns of life;
In glory burns the victor's name,
    After strife.
Do your duty, never swerve —
    Smooth or rough —
Until God, whom all we serve,
    Says "Enough."
LUCELLA CLARK.

## WHAT GOD SEES.

WHEN the winter snow-flakes fall,
God in heaven can count them all;
When the stars are shining bright,
Out upon a frosty night,
God can tell them all the same,
God can give each star its name.

God in heaven can also see
Children in their play agree.
Never rude, or cross, or wild,
Always kind, forbearing, mild;
Angels from their homes of light
Gladly look on such a sight.

---

BAD Thought's a thief! he acts his part;
Creeps through the window of the heart;
And, if he once his way can win,
He lets a hundred robbers in.

## GOOD COUNSEL.

Guard, my child, thy tongue,
That it speak no wrong;
Let no evil word pass o'er it;
Set the watch of truth before it.
That it speak no wrong,
Guard, my child, thy tongue.

Guard, my child, thy eyes;
Prying is not wise;
Let them look on what is right;
From all evil turn their sight.

Guard, my child, thine ear;
Wicked words will sear;
Let no evil words come in
That may cause the soul to sin.

Ear, and eye, and tongue,
Guard while thou art young;
For, alas! these busy three
Can unruly members be.
Guard while thou art young,
Ears, and eyes, and tongue.

## HEROES.

The heroes are not all six feet tall;
Large souls may dwell in bodies small.
The heart that will melt with sympathy
For the poor and the weak, whoe'er it be,
Is a thing of beauty, whether it shine
In a man of forty or a lad of nine.

## THE LITTLE CORPORAL'S SONG.

BOLD as an arrow-stroke,
 Swift as the light,
Brave little hearts of oak,
 On for the right.

Life is a tented field —
 Soldiers are we;
Ne'er to the foeman yield —
 Dare to be free!

Free from the foes that kill
 All we most prize,
Fierce and ungoverned will,
 Hatred and lies.

Free from the silken chains
 Idleness weaves;
Free from the blush and pain
 Cowardice weaves.

Loyal and dutiful,
 True as the sun —
Heights of the beautiful
 Yet to be won.

Conscience on picket-guard,
 Hope in the rear;
Faith as our shield and ward,
 God ever near.

On, 'neath our starry flag,
 Fighting the wrong!
Hill-top and distant crag,
 Echo our song.

*From "The Little Corporal."*

## THE OLD LOVE.

I ONCE had a sweet little doll, dears,
　　The prettiest doll in the world.
Her cheeks were so red and so white, dears,
　　And her hair was so charmingly curled.
But I lost my poor little doll, dears,
　　As I played on the heath one day;
And I cried for her more than a week, dears,
　　But I never could find where she lay.

I found my poor little doll, dears,
　　As I played on the heath one day;
Folks say she is terribly changed, dears,
　　For her paint is all washed away;
And her arms trodden off by the cows, dears,
　　And her hair not the least bit curled;
Yet for old sake's sake she is still, dears,
　　The prettiest doll in the world.
　　　　　　　　　　CHARLES KINGSLEY.

## IS IT YOU?

THERE is a child — a boy or girl —
　　I'm sorry it is true —
Who doesn't mind when spoken to:
　　Is it? — It isn't you!
　　O no, it can't be you!

I know a child — a boy or girl —
　　I'm loathe to say I do —
Who struck a little playmate child:
　　Was it? — It wasn't you!
　　I hope that 'twasn't you!

I know a child — a boy or girl —
  I hope that such are few —
Who told a lie; yes, told a lie!
  Was it? — It wasn't you!
  It cannot be 'twas you!

There is a boy — I know a boy —
  I cannot love him though —
Who robs the little birdies' nests;
  Is it? — It can't be you!
  That bad boy can't be you!

A girl there is — a girl I know —
  And I would love her too,
But that she is so proud and vain;
  Is it? — It can't be you!
  That surely isn't you!
                           Mrs. Goodwin.

## LITTLE SUNBEAMS.

Kind words are little sunbeams,
  That sparkle as they fall;
And loving smiles are sunbeams,
  A light of joy to all.
In sorrow's eye they dry the tear,
And bring the fainting heart good cheer.

## KIND HEARTS.

Kind hearts are the gardens,
  Kind thoughts are the roots,
Kind words are the blossoms,
  Kind deeds are the fruits.

## WHO STOLE THE BIRD'S NEST?

"To-whit! To-whit! To-whee!
Will you listen to me?
Who stole four eggs I laid?"

"Not I," said the cow, "Moo-oo!
Such a thing I'd never do.
I gave you a whisp of hay,
But didn't take your nest away.
Not I," said the cow. "Moo-oo!
Such a thing I'd never do."

"Bobolink! Bobolink!
Now what do you think?
Who stole a nest away
From the plum-tree to-day?"

"Not I," said the dog; "Bow-wow!
I wouldn't be so mean anyhow!
I gave hairs the nest to make;
But the nest I did not take.
Not I," said the dog; "Bow-wow!
I'm not so mean anyhow!"

"Coo-coo! Coo-coo! Coo-coo!
Let me speak a word to you!
Who stole that pretty nest
From little yellow-breast?"

"Not I," said the sheep; "Oh, no!
I wouldn't treat a poor bird so.
I gave wool the nest to line;
But the nest was none of mine.

Baa! Baa!" said the sheep; "Oh, no!
I wouldn't treat a poor bird so!"

"Caw! Caw!" cried the crow;
"I should like to know
What thief took away
A bird's nest to-day."

"Cluck! Cluck!" said the hen,
"Don't ask me again!
Why, I haven't a chick
Would do such a trick.
We all gave her a feather,
And she wove them together.
I'd scorn to intrude
On her and her brood.
Cluck! Cluck!" said the hen;
"Don't ask me again!"

"Chirr-a-whirr! Chirr-a-whirr!
All the birds make a stir!
Let us find out his name,
And all cry, 'for shame!'"

"I would not rob a bird,"
Said little Mary Green;
"I think I never heard
Of anything so mean."

"It is very cruel, too,"
Said little Alice Neal;
"I wonder if he knew
How sad the bird would feel."

A little boy hung down his head,
And went and hid behind the bed;
For he stole that pretty nest
From poor little yellow-breast.
And he felt so full of shame,
He didn't like to tell his name.

LYDIA MARIA CHILD.

## I'LL TRY.

Two robin red-breasts built their nest
    Within a hollow tree;
The hen sat quietly at home,
    The cock sang merrily;
And all the little ones said,
    " Wee-wee! wee-wee! wee-wee!"

One day the sun was warm and bright,
    And shining in the sky;
Cock Robin said, " My little dears,
    'Tis time you learned to fly."
And all the little ones said,
    " I'll try! I'll try! I'll try!"

I know a child, and who she is
    I'll tell you by and by;
When mamma says, " Do this," or " that,"
    She says, " What for? " and " why? "
She'd be a better child by far
    If she would say, " I'll try."

## ANSWER TO A CHILD'S QUESTION.

Do you ask what the birds say? The sparrow, the dove,
The linnet, and thrush, say "I love and I love!"
In the winter they're silent, the wind is so strong;
What it says, I don't know, but it sings a loud song;
But green leaves and blossoms and sunny warm weather,
And singing and loving, all come back together;
But the lark is so brimful of gladness and love,
The green fields below him, the blue sky above,
That he sings, and he sings, and forever sings he,
"I love my love, and my love loves me."

S. T. COLERIDGE.

## THE MOON.

Oh, look at the moon!
    She is shining up there;
O mother, she looks
    Like a lamp in the air!

Last week she was smaller,
    And shaped like a bow;
But now she's grown bigger,
    And round as an O.

Pretty moon, pretty moon,
    How you shine on the door,
And make it all bright
    On my nursery floor!

You shine on my playthings,
    And show me their place;
And I love to look up
    At your pretty, bright face.

And there is a star
    Close by you; and may be
That small twinkling star
    Is your little baby.
Mrs. Follen.

## WE ARE BUT MINUTES.

We are but minutes — little things,
Each one furnished with sixty wings,
With which we fly on our unseen track,
And not a minute ever comes back.

We are but minutes — yet each one bears
A little burden of joys and cares.
Patiently take the minutes of pain —
The worst of minutes cannot remain.

We are but minutes — when we bring
A few of the drops from pleasure's spring,
Taste their sweetness while we stay —
It takes but a minute to fly away.

We are but minutes — use us well,
For how we are used we must one day tell;
Who uses minutes has hours to use —
Who loses minutes whole years must lose.

## THE PIPER AND CHILD.

PIPING down the valleys wild,
    Piping songs of pleasant glee,
On a cloud I saw a child,
    And he laughing, said to me:

"Pipe a song about a lamb."
    So I piped with merry cheer.
"Piper, pipe that song again."
    So I piped; he wept to hear.

"Drop thy pipe, thy happy pipe;
    Sing thy songs of happy cheer."
So I sang the same again,
    While he wept with joy to hear.

"Piper, sit thee down and write,
    In a book that all may read."
So he vanished from my sight,
    And I plucked a hollow reed,

And I made a rural pen;
    And I stained the water clear;
And I wrote my happy songs
    Every child may joy to hear.

                  WILLIAM BLAKE.

## LITTLE KEYS.

HEARTS, like doors, can ope with ease
    To very, very little keys;
And don't forget that two are these:
    "I thank you, sir," and "If you please."

## LITTLE THINGS.

Little drops of water,
    Little grains of sand,
Make the mighty ocean
    And the pleasant land.

Thus the little minutes,
    Humble though they be,
Make the mighty ages
    Of eternity.

So our little errors
    Lead the soul away
From the path of virtue,
    Oft in sin to stray.

Little deeds of kindness,
    Little words of love,
Make our earth an Eden,
    Like the heaven above.

---

A million little diamonds
    Twinkled on the trees;
And all the little maidens said,
    "A jewel, if you please!"

But while they held their hands outstretched,
    To catch the diamonds gay,
A million little sunbeams came
    And stole them all away.

## TRY, TRY AGAIN.

Here's a lesson all should heed —
    Try, try, try again!
If at first you don't succeed,
    Try, try, try again!
Let your courage well appear;
If you only persevere
You will conquer, never fear;
    Try, try, try again!

Twice or thrice though you should fail,
    Try again!
If at last you would prevail,
    Try again!
When you strive, there's no disgrace
Though you fail to win the race;
Bravely, then, in such a case,
    Try, try, try again!

Let the thing be e'er so hard,
    Try again!
Time will surely bring reward,
    Try again!
That which other folks can do,
Why, with patience, may not you?
    Try, try, try again!

## SEVEN TIMES ONE.

THERE'S no dew left on the daisies and clover,
    There's no rain left in heaven.
I've said my "seven times" over and over, —
    Seven times one are seven.

I am old, — so old I can write a letter;
    My birthday lessons are done.
The lambs play always, — they know no better;
    They are only one times one.

O moon! in the night I have seen you sailing
    And shining so round and low.
You were bright — ah, bright — but your light is fading;
    You are nothing now but a bow.

You moon! have you done something wrong in heaven,
    That God has hidden your face?
I hope, if you have, you will soon be forgiven,
    And shine again in your place.

O velvet bee! you're a dusty fellow, —
    You've powdered your legs with gold!
O brave marshmary-buds, rich and yellow,
    Give me your money to hold!

O columbine! open your folded wrapper,
    Where two twin turtle-doves dwell!
O cuckoo-pint! toll me the purple clapper
    That hangs in your clear green bell!

And show me your nest, with the young ones in it:
    I will not steal them away;
I am old! you may trust me, linnet, linnet!
    I am seven times one to-day.

JEAN INGELOW.

## LOVE ONE ANOTHER.

CHILDREN, do you love each other?
    Are you always kind and true?
Do you always do to others
    As you'd have them do to you?
Are you gentle to each other?
    Are you careful, day by day,
Not to give offence by actions
    Or by anything you say?

Little children, love each other,
    Never give another pain;
If your brother speak in anger,
    Answer not in wrath again.
Be not selfish to each other —
    Never mar another's rest,
Strive to make each other happy,
    And you will yourself be blest.

## THE DANDELION.

LITTLE gypsy Dandelion,
    Dancing in the sun,
Have you any curls to sell?
    "Not a single one!"
Have you any eggs and cheese
    To go a-marketing?
"I have neither one of these,
    For beggar or for king."

Little idle Dandelion,
    Then I'll mow you down;
What is it you're good for,
    With your golden crown?
"Oh, I gild the fields afar,
    In the pleasant spring,
Shining like the morning star,
    With the light I bring."
        MARY N. PRESCOTT, *from* "*St. Nicholas.*"

## EVERY LITTLE HELPS.

WHAT if a drop of rain should plead,
    "So small a drop as I
Can ne'er refresh the thirsty mead,
    I'll tarry in the sky"?

What if the shining beam of noon
    Should in its fountain stay,
Because its feeble light alone
    Cannot create a day?

Does not each raindrop help to form
    The cool, refreshing shower?
And every ray of light to warm
    And beautify the flower?

## GOVERN YOUR TEMPER.

HE who ruleth well his heart
    And keeps his temper down,
Acts a better, wiser part
    Than he who takes a town.

## LITTLE BY LITTLE.

While the new years come and the old years go,
How, little by little, all things grow!
All things grow, and all decay —
Little by little passing away.
Little by little, on fertile plain,
Ripen the harvests of golden grain,
Waving and flashing in the sun
When the summer at last is done.

Low on the ground an acorn lies —
Little by little it mounts to the skies,
Shadow and shelter for wandering herds,
Home for a hundred singing birds.
Little by little the great rocks grew,
Long, long ago, when the world was new;
Slowly and silently, stately and free,
Cities of coral under the sea
Little by little are builded, while so
The new years come and the old. years go.

Little by little all tasks are done,
So are the crowns of the faithful won,
So is heaven in our hearts begun.
With work and with weeping, with laughter and play,
Little by little the longest day
And the longest life are passing away —
Passing without return, while so
The new years come and the old years go.

Luella Clark.

## CHILDREN.

Come to me, O ye children!
    For I hear you in your play,
And the questions that perplexed me
    Have vanished quite away.

Ye open the eastern windows,
    That look towards the sun,
When thoughts are singing swallows
    And brooks of morning run.

In your hearts are the birds and the sunshine,
    In your thoughts the brooklets flow;
But in mine is the wind of Autumn
    And the first fall of the snow.

Ah! what would the world be to us
    If the children were no more?
We should dread the desert behind us
    Worse than the dark before.

What the leaves are to the forest,
    With light and air for food,
Ere their sweet and tender juices
    Have been hardened into wood, —

That to the world are children;
    Through them it feels a glow
Of a brighter and sunnier climate
    Than reaches the trunks below.

Come to me, O ye children!
    And whisper in my ear

What the birds and the winds are singing
   In your sunny atmosphere.

For what are all our contrivings,
   And the wisdom of our books,
When compared with your caresses,
   And the gladness of your looks?

Ye are better than all the ballads
   That ever were sung or said;
For ye are the living poems,
   And all the rest are dead.
                              LONGFELLOW.

# INTERMEDIATE CLASSES.

# Selections for Intermediate Classes.

## A GEM.

Once from a cloud, a drop of rain
    Fell, trembling, in the sea,
And when she saw the wide-spread main,
    Shame veiled her modesty:

"What place on this wide sea have I?
    What room is left for me?
Sure it were better that I die
    In this immensity!"

But while her self-abasing fear
    Its lowliness confessed,
A shell received and welcomed her,
    And pressed her to its breast.

And nourished there, the drop became
    A pearl for royal eyes —
Exalted by its lowly shame,
    And humbled but to rise!

## THE NEW YEAR.

It's coming, boys,
It's almost here;
It's coming, girls,
The grand New Year!
A year to be glad in,
Not to be bad in;
A year to live in,
To gain and give in;
A year for trying,
And not for sighing;
A year for striving
And hearty thriving;
A bright New Year.
Oh! hold it dear!
For God, who sendeth,
He only lendeth.
MARY MAPES DODGE.

## TRIP LIGHTLY OVER TROUBLE.

Trip lightly over trouble,
  Trip lightly over wrong;
We only make them double
  By dwelling on them long.

Trip lightly over sorrow;
  Though this day may be **dark**,
The sun will shine to-morrow,
  And gaily sing the lark.

## THE ROBIN'S SONG.

I ASKED a sweet robin, one morning in May,
Who sung in the apple tree over the way,
What it was he was singing so sweetly about,
For I'd tried a long while and I could not find out.

"Why, I'm sure," he replied, "you cannot guess wrong;
Don't you know I am singing a temperance song?
Teetotal, oh! that's the first word of my lay;
And then don't you see how I twitter away?

"'Tis because I have just dipped my beak in the spring,
And brushed the fair face of the lake with my wing;
Cold water! cold water! yes, that is my song,
And I love to keep singing it all the day long!"

## LOVING HEARTS.

NEVER a night so dark and drear,
   Never a cruel wind so chill,
But loving hearts can make it clear,
   And find some comfort in it still.
MARY MAPES DODGE.

HERE is a lesson that he who runs may read:
   Though I fear but few have won it, —
The best reward of a kindly deed
   Is the knowledge of having done it!
EDGAR FAWCETT.

## AN ENDURING NAME.

I WROTE my name upon the sand,
    And trusted it would stand for aye;
But soon, alas! the refluent sea
    Had washed my feeble lines away.

I carved my name upon the wood,
    And, after years, returned again:
I missed the shadow of the tree
    That stretched of old upon the plain.

To solid marble next my name
    I gave as a perpetual trust:
An earthquake rent it to its base,
    And now it lies o'erlaid with dust.

All these have failed. In wiser mood
    I turn and ask myself, "what then?
If I would have my name endure,
    I'll write it on the hearts of men,—

"In characters of living light,
    From kindly words and actions wrought;
And these, beyond the reach of time,
    Shall live immortal as my thought."

                      HORATIO ALGER.

---

IN works of labor, or of skill,
    I would be busy too,
For Satan finds some mischief still
    For idle hands to do.
                      WATTS.

## TRUST.

WE were crowded in the cabin,
    Not a soul would dare to sleep;
It was midnight on the waters,
    And a storm was on the deep.

'Tis a fearful thing in winter
    To be shattered by the blast,
And to hear the rattling trumpet
    Thunder, "Cut away the mast!"

So we shuddered there in silence,
    For the stoutest held his breath,
While the hungry sea was roaring,
    And the breakers talked with Death.

As thus we sat in darkness,
    Each one busy with his prayers,
"We are lost!" the captain shouted,
    As he staggered down the stairs.

But his little daughter whispered,
    As she took his icy hand,
"Isn't God upon the ocean,
    Just the same as on the land?"

Then we kissed the little maiden,
    And we spoke in better cheer;
And we anchored safe in harbor
    When the morn was shining clear.

JAMES T. FIELDS.

## A GOOD RULE.

'Tis well to walk with a cheerful heart
    Wherever our fortunes call,
With a friendly glance and an open hand
    And a gentle word for all.

Since life is a thorny and difficult path,
    Where toil is the portion of man,
We all should endeavor, while passing along,
    To make it as smooth as we can.

## DEEDS OF KINDNESS.

Suppose a glistening dew-drop
    Upon the grass should say,
"What can a little dew-drop do?
    I'd better roll away;"
The blade on which it rested,
    Before the day was done,
Without a drop to moisten it,
    Would wither in the sun.

How many deeds of kindness
    A little child may do,
Although it has so little strength,
    And little wisdom too.
It wants a loving spirit,
    Much more than strength, to prove
How many things a child may do
    For strength by his love.

## KINDNESS.

I WOULD not hurt a living thing,
    However weak or small;
The beasts that graze, the birds that sing,
    Our Father made them all;
Without His notice, I have read,
    A sparrow cannot fall.

## TOBACCO.

TOBACCO, an outlandish weed,
Doth in the land strange wonders breed;
It taints the breath, the blood it dries,
It burns the head, it blinds the eyes;
It dries the lungs, scourgeth the lights;
It 'numbs the soul, it dulls the sprites;
It brings a man into a maze,
And makes him sit for others' gaze;
It mars a man, it mars a purse,
A lean one fat, a fat one worse;
A white man black, a black man white,
A night a day, a day a night;
It turns the brain, like cat in pan,
And makes a Jack a gentleman.
                        FAIRHOLT.

PAY good heed, all ye who read,
    And beware of saying, "I can't";
'Tis a cowardly word, and apt to lead
    To idleness, folly, and want.
                        ELIZA COOK.

## THE PARTS OF SPEECH.

Three little words you often see,
Are articles — a, an, and the;
A noun's the name of anything,
As school, or garden, hoop, or swing;
Adjectives tell the kind of noun,
As great, small, pretty, white, or brown;
Instead of nouns, the pronouns stand —
Her head, his face, your arm, my hand;
Verbs tell of something to be done,
To read, count, sing, laugh, jump, or run;
How things are done, the adverbs tell,
As slowly, quickly, ill, or well!
Conjunctions join the words together,
As men and women, wind or weather;
The preposition stands before
A noun, as in or through a door;
The interjection shows surprise,
As oh! How pretty! Ah! How wise!
The whole are called nine parts of speech,
Which reading, writing, speaking teach.

---

Take hold, my son, of the toughest knots in life, and try to untie them; try to be worthy of man's highest estate; have high, noble, manly honor. There is but one test of everything, and that is, Is it right? If it is not, turn away from it.

Henry A. Wise.

## THE BAREFOOT BOY.

BLESSINGS on thee, little man,
Barefoot boy, with cheek of tan!
With thy turned-up pantaloons,
And thy merry-whistled tunes;
With thy red lip, redder still,
Kissed by strawberries on the hill;
With the sunshine on thy face,
Through thy torn brim's jaunty grace!
From my heart I give thee joy:
I was once a barefoot boy.
Prince thou art — the grown up man
Only is republican.
Let the million-dollard ride!
Barefoot, trudging at his side,
Thou hast more than he can buy,
In the reach of ear and eye:
Outward sunshine, inward joy;
Blessings on thee, barefoot boy!
J. G. WHITTIER.

## BEGINNING OF VICE.

A LITTLE theft, a small deceit,
    Too often leads to more;
'Tis hard at first, but tempts the feet
    As through an open door.
Just as the broadest rivers run
    From small and distant springs,
The greatest crimes that men have done,
    Have grown from little things.

## THISTLE-DOWN.

A FAIRY bit of thistle-down
Lodged in the middle of a town.
A few years sped; in each bare space
A thistle had found growing place, —
A million stubborn, bristling things
From one small seed with filmy wings.

A maiden, idling with a friend,
Uttered a jest, — nor dreamed the end;
And when ill-rumors filled the air,
Wondered all simply who could bear
To give such pain. Nor dreamed her jest
Had been the text for all the rest.

HENRIETTA R. ELIOT, in " St. Nicholas."

## SPEAK THE TRUTH.

BOY, at all times tell the truth,
Let no lie defile thy mouth;
If thou'rt wrong, be still the same —
Speak the truth and bear the blame.

Truth is honest, truth is sure;
Truth is strong and must endure;
Falsehood lasts a single day,
Then it vanishes away.

Boy, at all times tell the truth,
Let no lies defile thy mouth;
Truth is steadfast, sure, and fast —
Certain to prevail at last.

## SONG OF LIFE.

A TRAVELLER on a dusty road
    Strewed acorns on the lea;
And one took root and sprouted up,
    And grew into a tree.
Love sought its shade at evening-time,
    To breathe its early vows;
And Age was pleased, in heights of noon,
    To bask beneath its boughs.
The dormouse loved its dangling twigs,
    The birds sweet music bore —
It stood a glory in its place,
    A blessing evermore.

A little spring had lost its way
    Amid the grass and fern;
A passing stranger scooped a well
    Where weary men might turn.
He walled it in, and hung with care
    A ladle on the brink;
He thought not of the deed he did,
    But judged that toil might drink.
He passed again; and lo! the well,
    By summer never dried,
Had cooled ten thousand parchèd tongues,
    And saved a life beside.

A nameless man, amid the crowd
    That thronged the daily mart,
Let fall a word of hope and love,
    Unstudied from the heart,

A whisper on the tumult thrown,
    A transitory breath,
It raised a brother from the dust,
    It saved a soul from death.
O germ! O fount! O word of love!
    O thought at random cast!
Ye were but little at the first,
    But mighty at the last.
CHARLES MACKAY.

## A CHILD'S THOUGHT OF GOD.

THEY say that God lives very high;
    But if you look above the pines
You cannot see our God; and why?

And if you dig down in the mines,
    You never see Him in the gold;
Though from Him all that's glory shines.

God is so good, He wears a fold
    Of heaven and earth across His face —
Like secrets kept for love untold.

But, still I feel that His embrace
    Slides down by thrills through all things made.
Through sight and sound of every place.

As if my tender mother laid
    On my shut lips her kisses' pressure,
Half waking me at night, and said,
    "Who kissed you through the dark, dear
        guesser?"
MRS. BROWNING.

## NO ACT FALLS FRUITLESS.

Scorn not the slightest word or deed,
  Nor deem it void of power;
There's fruit in each wind-wafted seed
  That waits its natal hour.
A whispered word may touch the heart,
  And call it back to life;
A look of love bid sin depart,
  And still unholy* strife.
No act falls fruitless; none can tell
  How vast its powers may be,
Nor what results enfolded dwell
  Within it silently.
Work on, despair not; bring thy mite,
  Nor care how small it be;
God is with all that serve the right,
  The holy, true, and free.

---

Whatever hath been written shall remain,
Nor be erased, nor written o'er again;
The unwritten only still belongs to thee:
Take heed, and ponder well what that shall be.
Longfellow.

---

Be good, sweet maid, and let who will be clever;
  Do noble things, not dream them, all day long;
And so make life, death, and that vast forever
  One grand, sweet song.
Charles Kingsley.

## THE POWER OF LITTLES.

GREAT events, we often find,
    On little things depend,
And very small beginnings
    Have oft a mighty end.

Letters joined make words,
    And words to books may grow,
As flake on flake descending
    Forms an avalanche of snow.

A single utterance may good
    Or evil thought inspire;
One little spark enkindled
    May set a town on fire.

What volumes may be written
    With little drops of ink!
How small a leak, unnoticed,
    A mighty ship will sink.

A tiny insect's labor
    Makes the coral strand,
And mighty seas are girdled
    With grains of golden sand.

A daily penny, saved,
    A fortune may begin;
A daily penny, squandered,
    May lead to vice and sin.

Our life is made entirely
    Of moments multiplied,

As little streamlets, joining,
  Form the ocean's tide.

Our hours and days, our months and years,
  Are in small moments given.
They constitute our time below,
  Eternity in heaven.

## HAROUN AL RASCHID.

ONE day, Haroun Al Raschid read
A book wherein the poet said:

"Where are the kings, and where the rest
Of men who once the world possessed?

"They're gone with all their pomp and show,
They're gone the way thou shalt go."

"O thou who choosest for thy share
The world, and what the world calls fair,

"Take all that it can give or lend,
But know that death is at the end!"

Haroun Al Raschid bowed his head;
Tears fell upon the page he read.
                                    LONGFELLOW.

WHENE'ER a duty waits for thee,
  With some judgment view it,
And never idly wish it done, —
  Begin at once and do it.

## THE SANDS O' DEE.

"Go, Mary, go and call the cattle home,
    And call the cattle home,
And call the cattle home,
    Across the sands o' Dee."
The western wind was wild and dank with foam,
    And all alone went she.

The creeping tide came up along the sand,
    And o'er and o'er the sand,
And round and round the sand,
    As far as eye could see;
The blinding mist came down and hid the land—
    And never home came she.

"Oh, is it weed, or fish, or floating hair—
    And tress o' golden hair,
O' drowned maiden's hair,
    Above the nets at sea?
Was never salmon yet that shone so fair,
    Among the stakes o' Dee."

They rowed her in across the rolling foam,
    The cruel, crawling foam,
The cruel, hungry foam,
    To her grave beside the sea;
But still the boatmen hear her call the cattle home,
    Across the sands o' Dee.
CHARLES KINGSLEY.

---

Thou must thyself be true,
If thou the truth wouldst teach.

## RULES FOR GOOD HEALTH.

TAKE the open air,
    The more you take the better;
Follow nature's laws
    To the very letter.

Let the doctors go
    To the Bay of Biscay.
Let alone the gin,
    The brandy and the whiskey.

Freely exercise,
    Keep your spirits cheerful;
Let no dread of sickness
    Make you ever fearful;

Eat the simplest food,
    Drink the pure cold water,
Then you will be well,
    Or at least you ought to.

## DO THE RIGHT, AND SPEAK THE TRUTH.

CHILDREN, who read my lay,
This much I have to say:
Each day, and every day,
    Do what is right —
Right things in great and small;
Then, though the sky should fall,
Sun, moon, and stars, and all,
    You shall have all light.

This further would I say:
Be you tempted as you may,
Each day, and every day,
   Speak what is true —
True things in great and small;
Then, though the sky should fall,
Sun, moon, and stars, and all,
   Heaven would shine through.

Life's journey through and through and through,
Speaking what is just and true,
Doing what is right to do
   Unto one and all,
When you work and when you play,
Each day, and every day;
Then peace shall gild your way,
   Though the sky should fall.

ALICE CARY.

## SEVEN TIMES TWO.

You bells in the steeple, ring, ring out your changes,
   How many soever they be,
And let the brown meadow-lark's note, as he ranges,
   Come over, come over to me.

Yet bird's clearest carol, by fall or by swelling,
   No magical sense conveys;
And bells have forgotten their old art of telling
   The fortune of future days.

Poor bells! I forgive you; your good days are over:
   And mine, they are yet to be.

No listening, no longing shall aught, aught discover;
    You leave the story to me.

I wait for the day when dear hearts shall discover,
    While dear hands are laid on my head:
"The child is a woman, the book may close over,
    For all the lessons are said."

I wait for my story — the birds cannot sing it;
    Not one as he sits on the tree;
The bells cannot ring it; but long years, oh, bring it!
    Such as I wish it to be.

---

## KIND WORDS AND LOOKS.

A LITTLE word in kindness spoken,
    A motion, or a tear,
Has often healed the heart that's broken,
    And made a friend sincere.

A word, a look, has crushed to earth
    Full many a budding flower,
Which, had a smile but owned its birth,
    Would light life's darkest hour.

Then deem it not an idle thing
    A pleasant word to speak;
The face you wear, the thoughts you bring,
    A heart may heal or break.

M. D. C. COLESWORTHY.

## DO YOUR BEST.

WHATEVER work comes to your hand,
    At home or at your school,
Do your best with right good will;
    It is a golden rule.

For he who always does his best,
    His best will better grow;
But he who shirks or slights his task,
    He lets the better go.

What if your lesson should be hard?
    You need not yield to sorrow:
For he who bravely works to-day,
    His tasks grow light to-morrow.

---

HAND in hand with angels,
    Through the world we go;
Brighter eyes are on us
    Than we blind ones know.
Tenderer voices cheer us
    Than we deaf ones will own;
Never walking heavenward,
    Can we walk alone.
                  LUCY LARCOM.

---

IF e'er, in doing aught, you dread
    Disgrace, if others know it,
Then, dearest child, the only way
    Is for you not to do it.

## THE MOUNTAIN AND THE SQUIRREL.

The mountain and the squirrel
Had a quarrel,
And the former called the latter " Little Prig ! "
Bun replied,
" You are doubtless very big,
But all sorts of things and weather
Must be taken in together
To make up a year,
And a sphere:
And I think it no disgrace
To occupy my place,
If I'm not so large as you,
You are not so small as I,
And not half so spry;
I'll not deny you make
A very pretty squirrel track.
Talents differ; all is well and wisely put;
If I cannot carry forests on my back,
Neither can you crack a nut."
R. W. Emerson.

---

Tiny threads make up the web,
    Little acts make up life's span;
Would you ever happy be,
    Spin them rightly while you can.
When the thread is broken quite,
    Too late then to spin aright.

## THE FOUR-LEAVED CLOVER.

They tell the story of a man
  Who roamed the wide world over,
And spent his whole life trying
  To find a four-leaved clover.

For this once found would bring him peace
  And happiness forever,
And so he roamed and sought in vain;
  He found the treasure never.

Till, coming home, a tired old man,
  Discouraged and downhearted,
He threw himself upon the ground,
  But quick again upstarted,

For there, before his own house-door,
  And spread the whole field over,
Were growing fragrant bunches of
  The long-sought, four-leaved clover.

Dear heart, there comes the truest joy
  To those who seek it never;
And happiness, in duty's field,
  Rewards the doer ever.

N. Earle, in "*Youth's Companion.*"

## DO YOUR BEST.

Though your duty may be hard,
  Look not on it as an ill;
If it be an honest task,
  Do it with an honest will.

Do whate'er you have to do
  With a true and earnest zeal;
Bend your sinews to the task,
  Put your shoulder to the wheel.

Do your best, your very best,
  And do it every day;
You will all be sure to find
  That to be the wisest way.

## HONEST AND TRUE.

Not many can stand in the sunlight,
  'Neath skies ever arching and blue,
The children of fame and of fortune,
  But all can be honest and true.

To inherit the kingdom of beauty,
  May not be for me or for you;
It is much to be born in the purple,
  But 'tis more to be honest and true.

It is pleasant to stand with the highest,
  If it were only to share in their view;
To be friends with the best and the wisest,
  But 'tis more to be honest and true.

We may not be as wise a Solon,
  We may not be "rich as a Jew,"
Or as grand as a king or a sultan,
  But let us be honest and true.

C. B. HEATH, in "*Youth's Companion.*"

## ADVICE TO BOYS.

Whatever you are, be brave;
The liar's a coward and slave,
    Though clever at ruses
    And sharp at excuses,
He's a sneaking and pitiful knave.

Whatever you are, be frank;
'Tis better than money and rank
    Still cleave to the right,
    Be lovers of light,
Be open, above board, and frank.

Whatever you are, be kind;
Be gentle in manners and mind.
    The man gentle in mien,
    Words, and temper, I ween,
Is the gentleman truly refined.

## DRIVE THE NAIL ARIGHT.

Drive the nail aright, boys,
    Hit it on the head;
Strike with all your might, boys,
    While the iron's red.

When you've work to do, boys,
    Do it with a will;
They who reach the top, boys,
    First must climb the hill.

Standing at the foot, boys,
    Gazing at the sky,

How can you get up, boys,
  If you never try?
Though you stumble oft, boys,
  Never be downcast;
Try, and try again, boys —
  You'll succeed at last.

## SPEAK GENTLY.

Speak gently; it is better far
  To rule by love than fear;
Speak gently; let no harsh words mar
  The good we might do here.

Speak gently to the little child;
  Its love be sure to gain;
Teach it in accents soft and mild;
  It may not long remain.

Speak gently to the aged one,
  Grieve not the care-worn heart;
The sands of life are nearly run:
  Let such in peace depart.

Speak gently, kindly, to the poor;
  Let no harsh word be heard:
They have enough they must endure,
  Without an unkind word.

Speak gently to the erring; know
  They may have toiled in vain:
Perhaps unkindness made them so —
  Oh, win them back again!

Speak gently; 'tis a little thing
    Dropped in the heart's deep well;
The good, the joy, which it may bring,
    Eternity shall tell.

## THE BROOK.

I CHATTER, chatter, as I flow
    To join the brimming river;
For men may come and men may go,
    But I go on forever.

I wind about, and in and out,
    With here a blossom sailing,
And here and there a lusty trout,
    And here and there a grayling.

I steal by lawns and grassy plots,
    I slide by hazel covers,
I move the sweet forget-me-nots
    That grow for happy lovers.

I slip, I slide, I gloom, I glance,
    Among my skimming swallows;
I make the netted sunbeams dance
    Against my sandy shallows.

I murmur under moon and stars;
    I bound by wildernesses;
I linger by my shingly bars;
    I loiter round my cresses.

And out again I curve and flow
    To join the brimming river,
For men may come and men may go,
    But I go on forever.
                    TENNYSON.

## THE OAK.

The oak-tree boughs once touched the grass;
    But every year they grew
A little farther from the ground,
    And nearer toward the blue.

So live that you each year may be,
    While time glides swiftly by,
A little farther from the earth,
    And nearer to the sky.

## NEVER SAY FAIL!

Keep pushing — 'tis wiser
    Than sitting aside,
And dreaming and sighing
    And waiting the tide.
In life's earnest battle
    They only prevail,
Who daily march onward
    And never say fail!

With an eye ever open,
    A tongue that's not dumb,
And a heart that will never
    To sorrow succumb —
You'll battle and conquer
    Though thousands assail:
How strong and how mighty
    Who never say fail!

In life's early morning,
  In manhood's firm pride,
Let this be the motto
  Your footstep to guide;
In storm and in sunshine,
  Whatever assail,
We'll onward and conquer,
  And never say fail!

## DAYBREAK.

A WIND came up out of the sea,
And said, "O mists, make room for me."

It hailed the ships, and cried, "Sail on,
Ye mariners; the night is gone."

And hurried landward far away,
Crying, "Awake! it is the day."

It said unto the forest, "Shout!
Hang all your leafy banners out!"

It touched the wood-bird's folded wing,
And said, "O bird, awake and sing."

And o'er the farms, "O chanticleer,
Your clarion blow; the day is near."

It whispered to the fields of corn,
"Bow down, and hail the coming morn."

It shouted through the belfry-tower,
"Awake, O bell! proclaim the hour."

It crossed the churchyard with a sigh,
And said, "Not yet! in quiet lie."

LONGFELLOW.

## A GOOD NAME.

Oh that folk would well consider
    What it is to lose a name;
What this world is altogether,
    If bereft of honest fame.

Poverty ne'er brings dishonor,
    Hardship ne'er breeds sorrow's smart,
If bright conscience takes upon her
    To shed sunshine round the heart.

## NOBILITY.

True worth is in being, not seeming;
    In doing each day that goes by
Some little good — not in the dreaming
    Of great things to do by and by;
For whatever men say in blindness,
    And spite of the fancies of youth,
There's nothing so kingly as kindness,
    And nothing so royal as truth.

We get back our mete as we measure;
    We cannot do wrong and love right;
Nor can we give pain and get pleasure,
    For justice avenges each slight.
The air for the wing of the sparrow,
    The bush for the robin and wren;
But alway the path that is narrow
    And strait for the children of men.

Through envy, through malice, through hating,
    Against the world, early and late,
No jot of our courage abating,
    Our part is to work and to wait.
And slight is the sting of his trouble
    Whose winnings are less than his worth;
For he who is honest is noble,
    Whatever his fortunes or birth.
ALICE CARY.

## PRESS ON.

PRESS on! surmount the rocky steeps,
    Climb boldly o'er the torrent's arch;
He fails alone who feebly creeps;
    He wins who dares the hero's march;
Be thou a hero! let thy might
    Tramp on eternal snows its way,
And through the ebon walls of night,
    Hew down a passage unto day.
PARK BENJAMIN.

WE can never be too careful
    What the seed our hands shall sow;
Love from love is sure to ripen,
    Hate from hate is sure to grow.
Seeds of good or ill we scatter
    Heedlessly along our way;
But a glad or grievous fruitage
    Waits us at the harvest day.
Whatso'er our sowing be,
    Reaping, we its fruits must see.

## LITTLE BY LITTLE.

ONE step, and then another,
    And the longest walk is ended;
One stitch, and then another,
    And the largest rent is mended;
One brick upon another,
    And the highest wall is made;
One flake upon another,
    And the deepest snow is laid.

Then do not look disheartened
    O'er the work you have to do,
And say that such a mighty task
    You never can get through:
But just endeavor, day by day,
    Another point to gain,
And soon the mountain which you feared
    Will prove to be a plain.

---

THERE are as many lovely things,
    As many pleasant tones,
For those who sit by cottage hearths
    As those who sit on thrones.
                      MRS. HAWKESWORTH.

---

HE prayeth best who loveth best
    All things both great and small;
For the dear God who loveth us,
    He made and loveth all.         COLERIDGE.

## BY-AND-BY.

There's a little mischief-making
  Elfin, who is ever nigh,
Thwarting every undertaking;
  And his name is — By-and-by.

What we ought to do this minute
  "Will be better done," he'll cry,
If to-morrow we begin it.
  "Put it off," says By-and-by.

Those who heed the treacherous wooing
  Will his faithless guidance rue:
What we always put off doing,
  Clearly, we shall never do.

We shall reach what we endeavor,
  If on "Now" we more rely;
But unto the realms of never,
  Leads the pilot By-and-by.

## I CAN AND I WILL.

"I can!" he is a fiery youth;
  And "Will," a brother twin;
And arm in arm, in love and truth,
  They'll either die or win.

Shoulder to shoulder, ever ready,
  All firm and fearless, still
The brothers labor — true and steady —
  "I can" and brave "I will."

"I can" climbs to the mountain top,
    And plows the billowy main;
He lifts the hammer in the shop,
    And drives the saw and plane.

Then say "I can"! Yes, let it ring!
    There is a volume there;
There's meaning in the eagle's wing; —
    Then soar, and do, and dare.

Oh, banish from you every "can't,"
    And show yourself a man;
And nothing will your purpose daunt
    Led by the brave "I can."

## THE PSALM OF LIFE.

TELL me not in mournful numbers,
    Life is but an empty dream!
For the soul is dead that slumbers,
    And things are not what they seem.

Life is real! Life is earnest!
    And the grave is not its goal;
Dust thou art, to dust returnest,
    Was not spoken of the soul.

Not enjoyment and not sorrow,
    Is our destined end and way;
But to act, that each to-morrow
    Find us farther than to-day.

Art is long, and Time is fleeting,
 And our hearts, though stout and brave,
Still like muffled drums are beating
 Funeral marches to the grave.

In the world's broad field of battle,
 In the bivouac of Life,
Be not like dumb driven cattle!
 Be a hero in the strife!

Trust no future, howe'er pleasant!
 Let the dead Past bury its dead!
Act, — act in the living Present!
 Heart within, and God overhead!

Lives of great men all remind us
 We can make our lives sublime;
And departing leave behind us
 Footprints on the sands of time; —

Footprints, that perhaps another,
 Sailing o'er life's solemn main
A forlorn and shipwrecked brother,
 Seeing, shall take heart again.

Let us then be up and doing,
 With a heart for any fate;
Still achieving, still pursuing,
 Learn to labor and to wait.

LONGFELLOW.

# ADVANCED CLASSES.

# SELECTIONS FOR ADVANCED CLASSES.

## TRUST.

OH, yet we trust that somehow good
    Will be the final goal of ill,
    To pangs of nature, sins of will,
Defects of doubt and taints of blood;

That nothing walks with aimless feet;
    That not one life shall be destroyed,
    Or, cast as rubbish to the void,
When God hath made the pile complete;

That not a worm is cloven in vain;
    That not a moth with vain desire
    Is shrivelled in a fruitless fire,
Or but subserves another's gain.
              TENNYSON, *from* "*In Memoriam.*"

---

WESTWARD the star of empire takes its way,
    The first four acts already past,
The fifth shall end the drama with the day;
    Time's noblest offspring is the last.
              BISHOP GEORGE BERKLEY.

## NOBILITY.

FROM yon. blue heavens above us bent
The grand old gardener and his wife
   Smile at the claims of long descent.
Howe'er it be, it seems to me
   'Tis only noble to be good;
Kind hearts are more than coronets,
   And simple faith than Norman blood.
TENNYSON, from "Clara Vere de Vere."

## ACTION.

Do something! Do it soon! With all thy might;
   An angel's wing would droop if long at rest,
   And God inactive were no longer blest.
Some high or humble enterprise of good
   Contemplate till it shall possess thy mind,
Become thy study, pastime, rest, and food,
   And kindle in thy heart a flame refined:
Pray heaven for firmness thy whole soul to bind
   To this high purpose: To begin, pursue,
With thoughts all fixed, and feelings purely kind;
   Strength to complete, and with delight review,
   And strength to give the praise where all is due.
WILCOX.

THERE are points from which we can command our life,
Where the soul sweeps the future like a glass,
And coming things, full-freighted with our fate,
Jut out dark on the offing of the mind.
BAILEY, from "Festus."

## TRUE DIGNITY.

If thou be one whose heart the holy forms
Of young imagination have kept pure,
Stranger! henceforth be warned; and know that pride,
Howe'er disguised in its own majesty,
Is littleness; that he who feels contempt
For any living thing, hath faculties
Which he has never used; that thought with him
Is in its infancy. The man whose eye
Is ever on himself, doth look on one
The least of nature's works, one who might move
The wise man to that scorn which wisdom holds
Unlawful ever. O be wiser thou!
Instructed that true knowledge leads to love;
True dignity abides with him alone
Who, in the silent hour of universal thought,
Can still suspect, and still revere himself,
In lowliness of heart.
WORDSWORTH.

---

At summer eve, when heaven's aërial bow
Spans with bright arch the glittering hills below,
Why to yon mountain turns the musing eye,
Whose sunbright summit mingles with the sky?
Why do those cliffs of shadowy tint appear
More sweet than all the landscape shining near?
'Tis distance lends enchantment to the view,
And robes the mountain in its azure hue.
THOMAS CAMPBELL, from "Pleasures of Hope."

## CHEERFULNESS.

'Tis well to walk with a cheerful heart
  Wherever our fortunes call,
With a friendly glance, and an open hand,
  And a gentle word for all.

Since life is a thorny and difficult path,
  Where toil is the portion of man,
We all should endeavor, while passing along,
  To make it as smooth as we can.

## THE MEASURE OF LIFE.

We live in deeds, not years; in thoughts, not breaths;
In feelings, not in figures on the dial.
We should count time by heart-throbs, when they beat
For God, for man, for duty. He most lives,
Who thinks most, feels noblest, acts the best.
Life is but a means unto an end — that end,
Beginning, mean, and end to all things, God.

     PHILIP JAMES BAILEY, *from "Festus."*

I live for those who love me,
  For those who know me true;
For the heaven that smiles above me,
  And awaits my spirit too;
For the cause that lacks assistance,
For the wrongs that need resistance,
For the future in the distance,
  And the good that I can do.

     G. L. BANKS.

## TRUE DIGNITY.

Is there for honest poverty
    Wha hangs his head, and a' that?
The coward slave, we pass him by;
    We dare be poor for a' that.
For a' that, and a' that,
    Our toil's obscure, and a' that;
The rank is but the guinea's stamp —
    The man's the gowd for a' that.

A prince can make a belted knight,
    A marquis, duke, and a' that;
But an honest man's aboon his might —
    Guid faith, he maunna fa' that!
For a' that and a' that!
    Their dignities, and a' that;
The pith o' sense and pride o' worth
    Are higher ranks than a' that.

Then let us pray that come it may —
    As come it will for a' that —
That sense and worth, o'er a' the earth,
    May bear the gree, and a' that —
For a' that, and a' that,
    It's coming yet for a' that —
When man to man, the warld o'er,
    Shall brothers be for a' that!
                        Robert Burns.

---

If little labor, little are our gains;
Man's fortunes are according to his pains.
                                    Herrick.

## SELF-FORGETFULNESS.

"FORGET thyself," if thou would'st rise
From earth and higher good surprise;
" Forget thyself," if thou would'st love
And know the spring of life above.

Who loses self in brotherhood,
Forth-giving, ever gathers good;
And who for truth or right would die,
In falling, gains the victory.

---

To each his sufferings; all are men,
    Condemned alike to groan;
The tender for another's pain,
    The unfeeling for his own.
Yet, ah! why should they know their fate,
Since sorrow never comes too late,
    And happiness too swiftly flies?
Thought would destroy their paradise.
No more:—Where ignorance is bliss,
    'Tis folly to be wise.
THOMAS GRAY, from "A Distant View of Eton."

---

WE look before and after,
    And pine for what is not;
Our sincerest laughter ·
    With some pain is fraught.
Our sweetest songs are those that tell of saddest
    thought. SHELLEY.

## TEMPERANCE IN THOUGHT AND SPEECH.

PRUNE thou thy words; the thoughts control
    That o'er thee swell and throng:
They will condense within the soul,
    And change to purpose strong.

But he who lets his feelings run
    In soft, luxurious flow,
Shrinks when hard service must be done,
    And faints at every woe.

Faith's meanest deed more favor bears,
    Where hearts and wills are weighed,
Than brightest transports, choicest prayers,
    Which bloom their hour and fade.
                    J. H. NEWMAN.

---

MAN is his own star, and the soul that can
Render an honest and a perfect man,
Commands all light, all influence, all fate;
Nothing to him falls early or too late.
Our acts our angels are, or good, or ill,
Our fatal shadows that walk by us still.
                    JOHN FLETCHER.

---

LET us know
Our indiscretion sometimes serves us well,
When our deep plots do pall: and that should teach us
There's a divinity that shapes our ends,
Rough-hew them how we will.
                    SHAKESPEARE, "*Hamlet.*"

## LABOR.

LABOR is rest from the sorrows that greet us,
Rest from all petty vexations that meet us,
Rest from sin-promptings that ever entreat us,
Rest from world-sirens that lure us to ill.
Work, — and pure slumbers shall wait on thy pillow;
Work, — thou shalt ride over care's coming billow;
Lie not down wearied 'neath woe's weeping-willow;
Work with a stout heart and resolute will.
F. S. OSGOOD.

LOOKING down the ladder of our deeds,
    The rounds seem slender; all past work appears
Unto the doer faulty; the heart bleeds,
    And pale regret comes weltering in tears,
To think how poor our best has been, how vain,
Beside the excellence we would attain.
HENRY ABBEY.

A KINDLY act is a kernel sown,
    That will grow to a goodly tree,
Shedding its fruit when time has flown
    Down the gulf of eternity.
JOHN BOYLE O'REILLY.

DARKNESS before, all joy behind!
Yet keep thy courage, do not mind:
He soonest reads the lesson right
Who reads with back against the light!
GEORGE HOUGHTON.

## IMMORTALITY OF THE SOUL.

THE soul, secured in her existence, smiles
At the drawn dagger, and defies its point.
The stars shall fade away, the sun himself
Grow dim with age, and nature sink in years,
But thou shalt flourish in immortal youth,
Unhurt amidst the war of elements,
The wreck of matter, and the crush of worlds.
ADDISON.

## ONWARD.

ONWARD, onward, may we press
    Through the path of duty;
Virtue is true happiness,
    Excellence true beauty;
Minds are of celestial birth;
Make we then a heaven of earth.

Closer, closer let us knit
    Hearts and hands together,
Where our fireside comforts sit
    In the wildest weather;
Oh, they wander wide who roam
For the joys of life from home.
JAMES MONTGOMERY.

THOUHT is deeper than all speech;
Feeling, deeper than all thought;
Souls to souls can never teach
What unto themselves was taught.
C. P. CRANCH.

## TRUE LIVING.

He liveth long who liveth well;
    All else is life but flung away;
He liveth longest who can tell
    Of true things truly done each day.

Then fill each hour with what will last;
    Buy up the moments as they go:
The life above, when this is past,
    Is the ripe fruit of life below.

Sow love, and taste its fruitage pure;
    Sow peace, and reap its harvest bright;
Sow sunbeams on the rock and moor,
    And find a harvest-home of light.
H. Bonar.

## PERFECTION.

To gild refined gold, to paint the lily,
To throw a perfume on the violet,
To smooth the ice, or add another hue
Unto the rainbow, or with taper light
To seek the beauteous eye of heaven to garnish,
Is wasteful and ridiculous excess.
Shakespeare, "King Lear."

Small service is true service while it lasts;
    Of friends, however humble, scorn not one;
The daisy, by the shadow that it casts,
    Protects the lingering dewdrop from the sun.
Wordsworth.

## CONTENTMENT.

My mind to me a kingdom is;
    Such perfect joy therein I find
As far excels all earthly bliss
    That God or Nature hath assigned;
Though much I want that most would have,
Yet still my mind forbids to crave.

Content I live; this is my stay,—
    I seek no more than may suffice.
I press to bear no haughty sway;
    Look, what I lack my mind supplies.
Lo, thus I triumph like a king,
Content with that my mind doth bring.

I laugh not at another's loss,
    I grudge not at another's gain;
No worldly wave my mind can toss;
    I brook that is another's bane.
I fear no foe, nor fawn on friend;
I loathe not life, nor dread mine end.

My wealth is health and perfect ease;
    My conscience clear my chief defence;
I never seek by bribes to please
    Nor by desert to give offence.
Thus do I live, thus will I die;
Would all did so as well as I!

                                WILLIAM BYRD.

    HAPPY is the man whose good intentions have borne fruit in deeds, and whose evil thoughts have perished in the blossom. — SCOTT, "*Rob Roy.*"

## FREEDOM.

Stone walls do not a prison make,
    Nor iron bars a cage;
Minds innocent and quiet take
    That for an hermitage.
If I have freedom in my love,
    And in my soul am free,
Angels alone, that soar above,
    Enjoy such liberty.
                        RICHARD LOVELACE.

## FORTITUDE.

Oh, never from thy tempted heart
Let thine integrity depart;
When disappointment fills the cup,
Undaunted, nobly drink it up;
Truth will prevail, and justice show
Her tardy honors, sure though slow;
Bear on — bear bravely on!
                        LONGFELLOW.

What's hallowed ground? 'Tis what gives birth
To sacred thoughts in souls of worth!
Peace! Independence! Truth! Go forth
    Earth's compass round;
And your high priesthood shall make earth
    All hallowed ground.
                        THOMAS CAMPBELL.

## HUMANITY.

I WOULD not enter on my list of friends
(Though graced with polished manners and fine sense,
Yet wanting sensibility) the man
Who needlessly sets foot upon a worm.
An inadvertant step may crush the snail
That crawls at evening in the public path;
But he that has humanity, forewarned,
Will tread aside, and let the reptile live.
WILLIAM COWPER.

## CHARITY.

TRUST not to each accusing tongue,
    As most weak persons do;
But still believe that story false
    Which ought not to be true.
SAMUEL BUTLER.

## INTRINSIC MERIT.

A JEWEL is a jewel still,
    Though lying in the dust,
And sand is sand, though up to heaven
    'Tis by the tempest thrust.
*Oriental, translated by* W. R. ALGER.

NOTHING useless is or low;
    Each thing in its place is best;
And what seems but idle show
    Strengthens and supports the rest.

## HAVE HOPE.

There's never an always cloudless sky,
  There's never a vale so fair,
But over it sometimes shadows lie
  In a chill and songless air.

But never a cloud o'erhung the day,
  And flung its shadows down,
But on its heaven-side gleamed one ray,
  Forming a sunshine crown.
                              M. J. Savage.

## PROCRASTINATION.

Be wise to-day; 'tis madness to defer;
Next day the fatal precedent will plead;
Thus on, till wisdom is pushed out of life.
Procrastination is the thief of time;
Year after year it steals, till all are fled,
And to the mercies of a moment leaves
The vast concerns of an eternal scene.
                              Young.

Every day brings a ship,
Every ship brings a word;
Well for those who have no fear,
Looking seaward well assured
That the word the vessel brings
Is the word they wish to hear.
                       Ralph Waldo Emerson.

## THIS WILL PASS AWAY.

WHEN wafted on by fortune's breeze,
   In endless peace thou seem'st to glide,
Prepare betimes for rougher seas,
   And check the boast of foolish pride;
Though smiling joy is there to-day,
Remember, "this will pass away!"

When all the sky is draped in black,
   And beaten by tempestuous gales,
Thy shuddering ship seems all awrack,
   Then trim again thy tattered sails;
To grim despair be not a prey;
Bethink thee, "this will pass away!"

Then, O my son, be not o'er proud,
   Nor yet cast down; judge thou aright;
When skies are clear, expect the cloud;
   In darkness wait the coming light;
Whatever be thy fate to-day,
Remember "this will pass away!"
                    J. G. SAXE.

## COURTESY.

How sweet and gracious, even in common speech,
Is that fine sense which men call courtesy!
Wholesome as air and genial as the light,
Welcome in every clime as breath of flowers, —
It transmutes aliens into trusting friends,
And gives its owner passport round the globe.
                         J. T. FIELDS.

## NIGHT.

How beautiful is night!
A dewy freshness fills the silent air;
No mist obscures, nor cloud, nor speck, nor stain
   Breaks the serene of heaven;
   In full-orbed glory yonder moon divine
   Rolls through the dark blue depths.
   Beneath her steady ray
   The desert circle spreads.
Like the round ocean girdled with the sky.
   How beautiful is night!
SOUTHEY.

## COURAGE.

Droop not, though shame, sin, and anguish are around thee!
Bravely fling off the cold chain that hath bound thee!
Look to yon pure heaven smiling beyond thee!
Rest not content in thy darkness — a clod!
Work — for some good, be it ever so slowly;
Cherish some flower, be it ever so lowly;
Labor! — all labor is noble and holy;
Let thy great deeds be thy prayer to thy God.
H. S. OSGOOD.

Though the mills of God grind slowly,
  . Yet they grind exceeding small;
Though with patience he stands waiting,
  With exactness grinds he all.
LONGFELLOW.

## INDEPENDENCE.

HAIL, independence, hail! Heaven's next best gift,
To that of life and an immortal soul!
The life of life! What to the banquet high
And sober meal gives taste; to the bowed roof
Fair-dreamed repose, and to the cottage charms.
THOMSON.

## FREEDOM OF THE SOUL.

HIGH walls and huge the body may confine,
And iron gates obstruct the prisoner's gaze,
And massive bolts may baffle his design,
And vigilant keepers watch his devious ways;
But scorns the immortal mind such base control;
No chains can bind it and no cell inclose.
WM. LLOYD GARRISON.

    To splendor only do we live?
        Must pomp alone our thoughts employ?
    All, all that pomp and splendor give,
        Is dearly bought with love and joy.
*Ballad of "Armine and Elvira."*

A THING of beauty is a joy forever;
Its loveliness increases; it will never
Pass into nothingness; but still will keep
A bower quiet for us, and a sleep
Full of sweet dreams, and health, and quiet breathing.
KEATS.

## INGRATITUDE.

Blow, blow, thou winter wind!
Thou art not so unkind
    As man's ingratitude;
Thy tooth is not so keen,
Because thou art not seen,
    Although thy breath be rude.

Freeze, freeze, thou bitter sky;
Thou dost not bite so nigh
    As benefits forgot;
Though thou the waters warp,
Thy sting is not so sharp
    As friend remembered not.
                  Shakespeare, *"As You Like It."*

---

The year's at the spring,
And day's at the morn;
Morning's at seven;
The hill-side's dew pearled;
The lark's on the wing;
The snail's on the thorn;
God's in his heaven —
All's right with the world.
                    Robert Browning.

---

If all were rain and never sun,
    No bow could span the hill;
If all were sun and never rain,
    There'd be no rainbow still.
                    Christiana G. Rosetti.

## ALL'S WELL.

"ALL'S well!" In the warfare of life
    Does my soul like a sentinel stand,
Prepâred to encounter the strife,
    With well-burnished weapon in hand?
While the senses securely repose,
    And doubt and temptation have room,
Does the keen ear of conscience unclose?
    Does she listen and catch through the gloom:
        "All's well?"

"All's well!" — can I echo the word?
    Does faith with a sleepless control
Bid the peaceful assurance be heard
    In the questionless depths of the soul?
Then fear not, frail heart! — When the scars
    Of the brave-foughten combat are past,
Clear voices that fall from the stars
    Will quiet thee on to the last:
        "All's well!"
                MARGARET J. PRESTON.

ONLY a sweet and virtuous soul,
    Like seasoned timber, never gives;
But though the whole world turn to coal,
    Then chiefly lives.
                GEORGE HERBERT.

THE world goes up and the world goes down,
    And the sunshine follows the rain;
And yesterday's sneer and yesterday's frown
    Can never come over again. — CHARLES KINGSLEY.

## SUFFERING.

O LIFE, O death, O time,
 O grave where all things flow,
'Tis yours to make our lot sublime
 With your great weight of woe.

Though sharpest anguish hearts may wring,
 Though bosoms torn may be,
Yet suffering is a holy thing;
 Without it what were we?

RICHARD CHEVEVIX TRENCH.

No earth-born will
Could ever trace a faultless line;
 Our truest steps are human still;
To walk unswerving were divine.

Truants from love, we dream of wrath;
 O rather let us trust the more!
Through all the wanderings of the path,
 We still can see our Father's door!

O. W. HOLMES.

BOOKS are yours,
Within whose silent chambers treasure lies
Preserved from age to age; more precious far
Than that accumulated store of gold
And orient gems which, for a day of need,
The sultan hides deep in ancestral tombs.
These hoards of truth you can unlock at will.

WORDSWORTH.

## THE GOOD GREAT MAN.

WHAT wouldst thou have a good great man obtain?
Wealth, title, dignity, a golden chain?
Or heap of corses which his sword hath slain?
Goodness and greatness are not means, but ends.
Hath he not always treasures, always friends,
The good great man? Three treasures, — love, and light,
    And calm thoughts, equable as infant's breath;
And three fast friends, more sure than day and night:
    Himself, his Maker, and the angel Death.
S. T. COLERIDGE.

WHY lose we life in anxious cares
To lay in hoards for future years?
Can these, when tortured by disease,
Cheer our sick hearts, or purchase ease?
Can these prolong our gasp of breath,
Or calm the troubled hour of death?
GAY.

MEN at some time are masters of their fates;
The fault, dear Brutus, is not in our stars,
But in ourselves, that we are underlings.
SHAKESPEARE, "Julius Cæsar."

GARMENTS that have one rent in them are subject to be torn on every nail and every briar; and glasses that are once cracked are soon broken; such is man's good name once tainted with just reproach.
BISHOP HALL.

## MERCY.

The quality of mercy is not strain'd;
It droppeth as the gentle rain from heaven
Upon the place beneath: It is twice blessed;
It blesseth him that gives, and him that takes:
'Tis mightiest in the mightiest; it becomes
The throned monarch better than his crown:
His sceptre shows the force of temporal power,
The attribute to awe and majesty,
Wherein doth sit the dread and fear of kings;
But mercy is above his sceptered sway.
It is enthroned in the hearts of kings,
It is an attribute of God himself;
And earthly power doth then show likest God's
When mercy seasons justice.

SHAKESPEARE, "*Merchant of Venice.*"

---

It is by imitation, far more than by precept, that we learn everything; and what we learn thus we acquire not only more effectually, but more pleasantly. This forms our manners, our opinions, our lives.

BURKE.

---

The fullest and best ears of corn hang lowest towards the ground.

BISHOP REYNOLDS.

---

The block of granite which was an obstacle in the pathway of the weak, becomes a stepping-stone in the pathway of the strong.

CARLYLE.

## THE MAN I LOVE.

I LOVE the man whose only pride
  Is wisdom, virtue, right;
Who feels, if truth is e'er denied,
  His honor has a blight;
Who ne'er evades by look or sign —
  In weal or woe the same;
Methinks the glories are divine
  Which cluster round his name.
D. C. COLESWORTHY.

THE man that hath no music in himself,
Nor is not moved with concord of sweet sounds,
Is fit for treasons, stratagems, and spoils:
The motions of his spirit are dull as night,
And his affections dark as Erebus:
Let no such man be trusted.
SHAKESPEARE, "Merchant of Venice."

HE that hath light within his own clear breast
May sit i' the centre, and enjoy bright day;
But he that hides a dark soul and foul thoughts,
Benighted, walks under the mid-day sun;
Himself is his own dungeon.
MILTON.

HOPE springs eternal in the human breast;
Man never is, but always to be, blest;
The soul uneasy, and confined from home,
Rests and expatiates in a life to come.
POPE.

## GOD AND THE RIGHT.

THRICE blest is he to whom is given
    The instinct that can tell
That God is on the field when he
    Is most invisible.

Blest, too, is he who can divine
    Where real right doth lie,
And dares to take the side that seems
    Wrong to man's blindfold eye.

For right is right, since God is God;
    And right the day must win;
To doubt would be disloyalty,
    To falter would be sin!
                  F. W. FABER.

---

THE crow doth sing as sweetly as the lark,
When neither is attended; and I think,
The nightingale, if she should sing by day,
When every goose is cackling, would be thought
No better a musician than the wren.
How many things by season season'd are
To their right praise and true perfection!
            SHAKESPEARE, "*Merchant of Venice.*"

---

TRUTH crushed to earth shall rise again;
    The eternal years of God are hers;
But error wounded, writhes in pain,
    And dies among his worshippers.
                      BRYANT.

## POLONIUS' ADVICE.

SEE thou character. Give thy thoughts no tongue,
Nor any unproportioned thought his act.
Be thou familiar, but by no means vulgar.
Those friends thou hast, and their adoption tried,
Grapple them to thy soul with hoops of steel;
But do not dull thy palm with entertainment
Of each new-hatched, unfledged comrade. Beware
Of entrance to a quarrel, but, being in,
Bear 't that the opposed may beware of thee.
Give every man thy ear, but few thy voice;
Take each man's censure, but reserve thy judgment.
Costly thy habit as thy purse can buy,
But not expressed in fancy; rich, not gaudy;
For the apparel oft proclaims the man.
Neither a borrower nor a lender be;
For loan oft loses both itself and friend,
And borrowing dulls the edge of husbandry.
This above all: to thine own self be true,
And it must follow, as the night the day,
Thou canst not be false to any man.

SHAKESPEARE, "*Hamlet.*"

---

READING furnishes the mind only with materials of knowledge; it is thinking makes what we read ours. We are of the ruminating kind, and it is not enough to cram ourselves with a great load of collections; unless we chew them over again, they will not give us strength and nourishment.

LOCKE.

## THE MEASURE OF LIFE.

WHY should we count our life by years,
Since years are short and pass away!
Or, why by fortune's smiles or tears,
Since tears are vain, and smiles decay!
Oh, count by virtues — these shall last
When life's lame-footed race is o'er;
And these, when earthly joys are past,
May cheer us on a brighter shore.
MRS. HALE.

FOR 'tis the mind that makes the body rich;
And as the sun·breaks through the darkest clouds,
So honor peereth in the meanest habit.
What, is the jay more precious than the lark,
Because his feathers are more beautiful?
Or is the adder better than the eel,
Because his painted skin contents the eye?
SHAKESPEARE, "*Taming of the Shrew.*"

ALL common good has common price;
   Exceeding good, exceeding;
Christ bought the keys of paradise
   By cruel bleeding.
And every soul that wins a place
   Upon its hills of pleasure,
Must give its all, and beg for grace
   To fill the measure.
J. G. HOLLAND.

## THE VALUE OF LABOR.

WHATE'ER is excellent in art proceeds
From labor and endurance; deep the oak
Must sink in stubborn earth, its roots obscure,
That hopes to lift its branches to the skies;
Gold cannot gold appear, until man's toil
Discloses wide the mountain's hidden ribs,
And digs the dusky ore, and breaks and grinds
Its gritty parts, and laves in limpid streams
With oft repeated toil, and oft in fire
The metal purifies.
                                        DYER.

HAVE more than thou showest,
Speak less than thou knowest,
Lend less than thou owest,
Learn more than thou trowest,
Set less than thou throwest.
                    SHAKESPEARE, "*King Lear.*"

KINDNESS hath resistless charms;
    All things else but weakly move;
Fiercest anger it disarms,
    And clips the wings of flying love.
                          EARL OF ROCHESTER.

MISS not the occasion; by the forelock take
That subtle power, the never-halting time,
Lest a mere moment's putting off should make
Mischance almost as heavy as a crime.
                                    WORDSWORTH.

## THE EAGLE.

He clasps the crag with hooked hands,
Close to the sun in lonely lands;
Ring'd with the azure world he stands;
The wrinkled sea beneath him crawls;
He watches from his mountain walls,
And like a thunderbolt he falls.
TENNYSON.

This was the noblest Roman of them all.
All the conspirators, save only he,
Did that they did in envy of great Cæsar;
He only, in a general honest thought
And common good to all, made one of them.
His life was gentle; and the elements
So mixed in him, that Nature might stand up,
And say, to all the world, "This was a man!"
SHAKESPEARE, "Julius Cæsar."

Oh, many a shaft at random sent
Finds mark its archer little meant;
And many a word at random spoken
May soothe or wound a heart that's broken.
SCOTT.

Opportunity has hair in front, but behind she is bald; if you seize her by the forelock, you may hold her; but, if suffered to escape, not Jupiter himself can catch her again.
A LATIN PROVERB.

## IT MIGHT HAVE BEEN.

Of all sad words of tongue or pen,
The saddest are these: "It might have been!"
Ah, well! for us all some sweet hope lies
Deeply buried from human eyes;
And, in the hereafter, angels may
Roll the stone from its grave away!
J. G. Whittier.

---

There is a tide in the affairs of men,
Which, taken at the flood, leads on to fortune;
Omitted, all the voyage of their life
Is bound in shallows, and in miseries.
On such a full sea are we now afloat;
And we must take the current when it serves,
Or lose our ventures.
Shakespeare, "*Julius Cæsar.*"

---

They never fail who die
In a great cause: the block may soak their gore,
Their heads may sodden in the sun; their limbs
Be strung to city gates or castle walls; —
But still their spirit walks abroad. Though years
Elapse, and others share as dark a doom,
They but augment the deep and sweeping thoughts
Which overpower all others, and conduct
The world at last to freedom.
Byron.

---

The Persians say of noisy, unreasonable talk: "I hear the noise of the mill-stone, but I see no meal."

## THE FREEMAN.

How happy is he born and taught
    That serveth not another's will;
Whose armor is his honest thought,
    And simple truth his utmost skill!
This man is freed from servile bands,
    Of hope to rise, or fear to fall —
Lord of himself, though not of lands;
    And, having nothing, yet hath all.
Sir Henry Wotton.

I AM not covetous of gold,
Nor care I who doth feed upon my cost;
It yearns me not if men my garments wear;
Such outward things dwell not in my desires:
But if it be a sin to covet honor,
I am the most offending soul alive.
Shakespeare, "Henry IV."

Young men, you are the architects of your own fortunes. Rely upon your own strength of body and soul. Take for your star self-reliance. Think well of yourself. Strike out. Assume your own position. Rise above the envious and jealous. Fire above the mark you intend to hit. Energy, invincible determination, with a right motive, are the levers that move the world. Be generous. Be civil. Read the papers. Advertise your business. Make money, and do good with it. Love your God and fellow-men. Love truth and virtue. Love your country, and obey its laws.
President Porter.

## A GOOD NAME.

Good name, in man and woman, dear my lord,
Is the immediate jewels of their souls:
Who steals my purse, steals trash: 'Tis something, nothing;
'Twas mine, 'tis his, and has been slave to thousands;
But he that filches from me my good name,
Robs me of that which not enriches him,
And makes me poor indeed.
SHAKESPEARE, "*Othello.*"

Not in the clamor of the crowded street,
  Not in the shouts and plaudits of the throng,
But in ourselves, are triumph and defeat.
LONGFELLOW, *Sonnet on* "*The Poets.*"

Freedom's battle, once begun,
Bequeathed from bleeding sire to son,
Though baffled oft is ever won.
BYRON.

There are two things in life that a sage must preserve at every sacrifice,—the coat of his stomach and the enamel of his teeth. Some evils admit of consolations: there are no comforters for dyspepsia and the toothache. BULWER LYTTON.

Some men are born great, some achieve greatness. and some have greatness thrust upon them.
SHAKESPEARE, "*Twelfth Night.*"

## A VISION OF THE FUTURE.

For I dipt into the future, far as human eye could see;
Saw the vision of the world and all the wonders that would be:

Saw the heavens fill with commerce, argosies of magic sails,
Pilots of the purple twilight, dropping down with costly bales:

Heard the heavens fill with shouting, and there rained a ghastly hue,
From the nations airy navies grappling in the central blue;

Far along the world-wide whispers of the south wind rushing warm,
With the standards of the peoples plunging through the thunder-storm,

Till the war drum throbbed no longer, and the battle-flags were furled
In the parliament of man, the federation of the world.

There the common sense of most shall hold a fretful realm in awe,
And the kindly earth shall slumber, rapt in universal law.

Tennyson, " *Locksley Hall.*"

---

Sweet are the uses of adversity,
Which, like the toad, ugly and venomous,
Wears yet a precious jewel in his head.

Shakespeare, "*As You Like It.*"

## GRADATIM.

HEAVEN is not reached at a single bound,
    But we build the ladder by which we rise
    From the lowly earth to the vaulted skies,
And we mount to its summit round by round.

I count this thing to be grandly true:
    That a noble deed is a step toward God, —
    Lifting the soul from the common clod
To a purer air and a broader view.

We rise by the things that are under feet;
    By what we have mastered of good and gain;
    By the pride deposed and the passion slain,
And the vanquished ills that we hourly meet.
J. G. HOLLAND.

---

WHAT a piece of work is man! How noble in reason! How infinite in faculty! In form and moving how express and admirable! In action how like an angel! In apprehension how like a god! The beauty of the world! The paragon of animals!
SHAKESPEARE, "Hamlet."

---

THE heights by great men reached and kept
    Were not attained by sudden flight,
But they, while their companions slept,
    Were toiling upward through the night.
LONGFELLOW.

---

KNOW how to listen, and you will profit even from those who talk badly.     PLUTARCH.

## THE SONG OF NATURE.

The leaf-tongues of the forest, the flower-lips of the sod,
The happy birds that hymn their rapture in the ear of God,
The summer wind that bringeth music over land and sea,
Have each a voice that singeth this sweet song of songs to me:
This world is full of beauty, like other worlds above;
And, if we did our duty, it might be full of love.
Gerald Massey.

What is a man,
If his chief good and market of his time
Be but to sleep and feed? A beast, no more.
Sure he that made us with such large discourse,
Looking before and after, gave us not
That capability and godlike reason
To rust in us unused.
Shakespeare, "*Hamlet.*"

Beautiful is young enthusiasm; keep it to the end, and be more and more correct in fixing on the object of it. It is a terrible thing to be wrong in that — the source of all our miseries and confusions whatever.
Carlyle.

True politeness is perfect ease and freedom. It simply consists in treating others just as you love to be treated yourself.
Lord Chesterfield.

## KNOWLEDGE AND WISDOM.

KNOWLEDGE and wisdom, far from being one,
Have ofttimes no connection. Knowledge dwells
In heads replete with thoughts of other men;
Wisdom, in minds attentive to their own.
Knowledge, — a rude, unprofitable mass,
The mere materials with which wisdom builds, —
Till smoothed, and squared, and fitted to its place,
Does but encumber whom it seems to enrich!
Knowledge is proud that he has learned so much,
Wisdom is humble that he knows no more.
COWPER.

WHAT stronger breastplate than a heart untainted?
Thrice is he armed that hath his quarrel just;
And he but naked, though locked up in steel,
Whose conscience with injustice is corrupted.
SHAKESPEARE, "King Henry VI."

MEN give me the credit for genius; but all the genius I have lies in this: when I have a subject on hand I study it profoundly. The effect I make they call the fruit of genius; it is, however, the fruit of labor and thought.
ALEXANDER HAMILTON.

So nigh is grandeur to our dust,
So near is God to man,
When duty whispers low, " Thou must,"
The youth replies, " I can."
EMERSON.

## COLUMBIA.

Columbia, Columbia, to glory arise,
The queen of the world and child of the skies!
Thy genius commands thee; with rapture behold,
While ages on ages thy splendors unfold.
Thy reign is the last and the noblest of time,
Most fruitful thy soil, most inviting thy clime;
Let the crimes of the East ne'er encrimson thy name,
Be freedom, and science, and virtue thy fame.
Timothy Dwight.

My crown is in my heart, not on my head;
Not decked with diamonds and Indian stones,
Not to be seen: my crown is called content;
A crown it is that seldom kings enjoy.
Shakespeare.

Since trifles make the sum of human things,
And half our misery from our foibles spring,
Since life's best joys consist in peace and ease,
Although but few can serve, yet all may please,
O, let the ungentle spirit learn from hence,
A small unkindness is a great offence!
Moore.

We scatter seeds with careless hand,
   And dream we shall ne'er see them more;
      But for a thousand years
      Their fruit appears,
In weeds that mar the land,
   Or healthful store.
John Keble.

## THE AMERICAN FLAG.

WHEN freedom, from her mountain height,
    Unfurled her standard to the air,
She tore the azure robe of night,
    And set the stars of glory there!
She mingled with its gorgeous dyes
The milky baldric of the skies,
And striped its pure celestial white
With streakings of the morning light;
Then from his mansion in the sun,
She called her eagle bearer down,
And gave into his mighty hand
The symbol of her chosen land.

Flag of the free hearts'· hope and home,
    By angel hands to valor given,
Thy stars have lit the welkin dome,
    And all thy hues were born in heaven.
Forever float that standard sheet!
    Where breathes the foe but falls before us,
With freedom's soil beneath our feet,
    And freedom's banner streaming o'er us?
                  JOSEPH RODMAN DRAKE.

---

THE purest treasure mortal times afford
Is spotless reputation; that away,
Men are but gilded loam, or painted clay.
                SHAKESPEARE, "*King Richard III.*"

---

I HOLD him to be dead, in whom shame is dead.
                      PLAUTUS.

## THE SWORD.

THE sword! a name of dread; yet when
Upon the freeman's thigh 'tis bound, —
While for his altar and his hearth,
While for the land that gave him birth,
The war-drums roll, the trumpets sound, —
How sacred is it then!

---

FOR honor travels in a strait so narrow,
Where one but goes abreast; keep then the path;
For emulation hath a thousand sons,
That one by one pursue: if you give way,
Or hedge aside from the direct forthright,
Like to an entered tide they all rush by,
And leave you hindmost.
SHAKESPEARE, "Troilus and Cressida."

---

STAY, stay at home my heart, and rest;
Home-keeping hearts are happiest,
For those that wander they know not where
Are full of trouble, and full of care;
    To stay at home is best.
LONGFELLOW.

---

  O WAD some power the giftie gie us
  To see oursel's as others see us?
  It wad frae monie a blunder free us,
    And foolish notion :
  What airs in dress an' gait wad lea's us
    And e'en devotion.
BURNS.

## WHAT CONSTITUTES A STATE.

WHAT constitutes a state?
Not high-raised battlement or labored mound,
    Thick wall or moated gate;
Not cities proud with spires and turrets crowned;
    Not bays and broad-armed ports,
Where, laughing at the storm, rich navies ride;
    Not starred and spangled courts,
Where low-browed baseness wafts perfume to pride.
    No! — men, high-minded men,
With powers as far above dull brutes endued
    In forest, brake, or den,
As beasts excel cold rocks and brambles rude, —
    Men who their duties know,
And know their rights, and, knowing, dare maintain,
    Prevent the long-aimed blow,
And crush the tyrant while they rend the chain;
    These constitute a state;
And sovereign law, that state's collected will,
    O'er thrones and globes elate,
Sits empress, crowning good, repressing ill.
SIR WILLIAM JONES.

IF to do were as easy as to know what were good to do, chapels had been churches, and poor men's cottages princes' palaces. It is a good divine that follows his own instructions: I can easier teach twenty what were good to be done, than to be one of the twenty to follow mine own teaching.
SHAKESPEARE, "Merchant of Venice."

## THE FREEMAN.

He is the freeman whom the truth makes free,
And all are slaves beside. There's not a chain
That hellish foes confederate for his harm
Can wind around him, but he casts it off
With as much ease as Samson his green withes.
He looks abroad into the varied field
Of nature; and though poor, perhaps, compared
With those whose mansions glitter in his sight,
Calls the delightful scenery all his own.
His are the mountains, and the valleys his,
And the resplendent rivers. His to enjoy
With a propriety that none can feel,
But who, with filial confidence inspired,
Can lift to heaven an unpresumptuous eye,
And smiling say, "My father made them all!"
Cowper.

Each, after all, learns only what he can;
Who grasps the moment as it flies,
He is the real man.
Goethe.

Intemperance wipes out God's image, and stamps it with the counterfeit die of the devil; intemperance smites a healthy body with disease from head to heel, and makes it more loathsome than the leprosy of Naaman or the sores of Lazarus; intemperance dethrones man's reason, and hides her bright beams in the mystic clouds that roll round the shattered temple of the human soul, curtained by midnight.
John B. Gough.

## THE OLD YEAR.

FULL knee-deep lies the winter snow,
   And the winter winds are wearily sighing:
Toll ye the church bell sad and slow,
And tread softly and speak low,
   For the old year lies a-dying.
   Old year, you must not die:
      You came to us so readily,
      You lived with us so steadily,
   Old year, you shall not die.
                             TENNYSON.

---

O WHO can hold a fire in his hand,
By thinking on the frosty Caucasus?
Or cloy the hungry edge of appetite,
By bare imagination of a feast?
Or wallow naked in December snow,
By thinking on fantastic summer's heat?
O no, the apprehension of the good
Gives but the greater feeling to the worse.
               SHAKESPEARE, "*King Richard II.*"

---

THE clear conception, outrunning the deductions of logic, the high purpose, the dauntless spirit, speaking on the tongue, beaming from the eye, informing every feature, and urging the whole man onward, right onward, to his object, — this, this is eloquence, or rather it is something greater and higher than all eloquence, — it is action, noble, sublime, godlike action.
                                                WEBSTER.

## ENCOURAGEMENT.

On! from honor unto honor; let not praise nor pelf
    allure!
Onward, upward, be thy course, and let thy foot be
    firm and sure.

On the earth are lands untrodden; somewhere under-
    neath the sun
Azure heights yet unascended, palmy countries to be
    won.

In the heart's diviner regions there are thoughts that
    stir the soul,
Till it shoots the bounds of darkness, past where stars
    and planets roll.

Life, in all its sunny aspects, all the moods of vice and
    pain,
Lie before thee. O, be certain nothing need be sought
    in vain.
                                BARRY CORNWALL.

---

    FULL fathom five thy father lies;
        Of his bones are coral made;
    These are pearls that were his eyes.
        Nothing of him that doth fade,
    But doth suffer a sea change
    Into something rich and strange.
    Sea-nymphs hourly ring his knell:
    Hark! Now I hear them, — ding-dong bell.
            SHAKESPEARE, *Ariel's Song in " The Tempest."*

## TRUE REST.

SWEET is the pleasure
    Itself cannot spoil!
Is not true leisure
    One with true toil?

Thou that wouldst taste it,
    Still do thy best;
Use it, not waste it. —
    Else 'tis no rest.

Rest is not quitting
    The busy career;
Rest is the fitting
    Of self to its sphere.

'Tis loving and serving
    The highest and best;
'Tis onwards! unswerving, —
    And that is true rest.
                    JOHN SULLIVAN DWIGHT.

---

No man is born into the world whose work
Is not born with him; there is always work,
And tools to work withal, for those who will;
And blessed are the horny hands of toil.
                                    LOWELL.

---

HONOR is like the eye, which cannot suffer the least impurity without damage; it is a precious stone, the price of which is lessened by the least flaw.
                                    BOSSUET.

## THE VOYAGE OF LIFE.

AND thou must sail upon this sea, a long
Eventful voyage. The wise may suffer wreck,
The foolish must. O, then be early wise!
Learn from the mariner his skilful art,
To ride upon the waves, and catch the breeze,
And dare the threatening storm, and trace a path
'Mid countless dangers, to the destined port,
Unerringly secure. O, learn from him
To station quick-eyed prudence at the helm,
To guard thy sail from passion's sudden blasts,
And make religion thy magnetic guide,
Which, though it trembles as it lowly lies,
Points to the light that changes not, in heaven!
HENRY WARE, JR.

HE who will not work shall want,
　　Nought for nought is just —
Won't do, must do when he can't;
　　Better rub than rust;
　　Bees are flying, sloth is dying,
　　Better rub than rust.
EBENEZER ELLIOT.

CANST thou not minister to a mind diseased,
Pluck from the memory a rooted sorrow,
Raze out the written troubles of the brain
And with some sweet oblivious antidote
Cleanse the stuff'd bosom of that perilous stuff
Which weighs upon the heart?
SHAKESPEARE, "Macbeth."

## WOLSEY'S ADVICE.

CROMWELL, I charge thee, fling away ambition:
By that sin fell the angels: how can man, then,
The image of his maker, hope to win by't?
Love thyself last; cherish those hearts that hate thee;
Corruption wins not more than honesty:
Still in thy right hand carry gentle Peace,
To silence envious tongues. Be just and fear not.
Let all the ends thou aim'st at be thy country's,
Thy God's, and Truth's; then, if thou fall'st, O Cromwell,
Thou fall'st a blessed martyr!
SHAKESPEARE, "*Henry VIII.*"

---

'TIS well to walk with a cheerful heart
    Wherever our fortunes call,
With a friendly glance and an open hand,
    And a gentle word for all.
Since life is a thorny and difficult path,
    Where toil is the portion of man,
We all should endeavor, while passing along,
    To make it as smooth as we can.

---

THEY whose hearts are whole and strong,
    Loving holiness,
Living clean from soil of wrong,
    Wearing truth's white dress, —
They unto no far-off height
    Wearily need climb;
Heaven to them is close in sight
    From these shores of time.    LUCY LARCOM.

## TO A WATERFOWL.

WHITHER, midst falling dew,
While glow the heavens with the last steps of day,
Far through their rosy depths dost thou pursue
    Thy solitary way?

Vainly the fowler's eye
Might mark thy distant flight to do thee wrong,
As, darkly painted on the crimson sky,
    Thy figure floats along.

. . . . . .

There is a power whose care
Teaches thy way along that pathless coast, —
The desert and illimitable air, —
    Lone wandering, but not lost.

. . . . . .

He, who from zone to zone,
Guides through the boundless sky thy certain flight,
In the long way I must tread alone
    Will lead my steps aright.

BRYANT.

IT is the mystery of the unknown
    That fascinates us; we are children still,
    Wayward and wistful; with one hand we cling
To the familiar things we call our own,
    And with the other, resolute of will,
    Grope in the dark for what the day will bring.
        LONGFELLOW, Sonnet on "The Two Rivers."

HE who has conferred a kindness should be silent, he who has received one should speak of it.

SENECA.

## FORBEARANCE.

If this great world of joy and pain
Revolve in one sure track,
If freedom, set, will rise again,
And virtue flown, come back,
Woe to the purblind crew who fill
The heart with each day's care,
Nor gain from past or future, skill
To bear and to forbear.
WORDSWORTH.

I DARE do all that may become a man;
Who dares do more is none.
SHAKESPEARE, "*Macbeth.*"

WHAT men want is not talent, it is purpose; not the power to achieve, but the will to labor.
BULWER LYTTON.

OUR ears should be accustomed to hear all manner of things, without carrying to the mind aught but good.
ERASMUS.

LOOK not mournfully into the past; it comes not back again. Wisely improve the present; it is thine. Go forth to meet the shadowy future without fear and with a manly heart.
LONGFELLOW.

Do good by stealth and blush to find it fame.
POPE.

## ACTION.

I AM a part of all that I have met;
Yet all experience is an arch where through
Gleams that untravelled world, whose margin fades
Forever and forever when I move.
How dull it is to pause, to make an end,
To rest unburnished, not to shine in use!
As tho' to breathe were life. Life piled on life
Were all too little, and of one to me
Little remains; but every hour is saved
From that eternal silence, something more,
A bringer of new things; and vile it were
For some three suns to store and hoard myself,
And this gray spirit yearning in desire
To follow knowledge, like a sinking star,
Beyond the utmost bound of human thought.

TENNYSON, " *Ulysses.*"

How far that little candle throws his beams!
So shines a good deed in a naughty world.

SHAKESPEARE, "*Merchant of Venice.*"

WHATEVER I have tried to do in my life, I have tried with all my heart to do well. What I have devoted myself to, I have devoted myself to completely. Never to put my hand to anything on which I would not throw my whole self, and never to affect depreciation of my work, whatever it was, I find now to have been my golden rules.

CHARLES DICKENS.

## FAREWELL TO LIFE.

Life! We've been long together,
Through pleasant and through cloudy weather;
'Tis hard to part when friends are dear —
Perhaps 'twill cost a sigh, a tear;
Then steal away, give little warning,
Choose thine own time;
Say not good night, — but in some brighter clime
Bid me good morning.
Mrs. Barbauld.

Ah! if our souls but poise and swing,
Like the compass in its brazen ring,
Ever level and ever true
To the toil and task we have to do,
We shall sail securely, and safely reach
The fortunate isles, on whose shining beach
The sights we see, and the sounds we hear
Will be those of joy and not of fear.
Longfellow, "*The Building of the Ship.*"

Defer not till to-morrow to be wise;
To-morrow's sun to thee may never rise.
Congreve.

It is dangerous to fall into impure conversation; when anything of the kind is said before you, if the place and person permit, reprove him that spoke; if that is not convenient, by your blushes and your silence show at least that you are displeased.
Epictetus.

## THE TOILER.

ROUND swings the hammer of industry, and quickly the
  sharp chisel rings,
And the heart of the toiler has throbbings that stir not
  the bosom of kings, —
He the true ruler and conqueror, he the true king of
  his race,
Who nerveth his arm for life's combat, and looks the
  strong world in the face.
DENIS FLORENCE MCCARTHY.

MY heart leaps up when I behold
  A rainbow in the sky;
So was it when my life began,
So is it now I am a man,
So be it when I shall grow old,
  Or let me die!
The child is father of the man;
And I could wish my days to be
Bound each to each by natural piety.
WORDSWORTH.

HE is ungrateful who denies that he has received a kindness which has been bestowed upon him; he is ungrateful who conceals it from others; he is ungrateful who makes no return for it; most ungrateful of all is he who forgets it.  CICERO.

IT is the characteristic of folly to discern the faults of others and to forget one's own.
CICERO.

## PERFECTION.

It is not growing like a tree
Or standing like a mark, three hundred year,
To fall a log at last, dry, bald and sear:
A lily of a day
Is fairer far in May,
Although it fall and die that night, —
It was the plant and flower of light.
In small proportions we just beauties see;
And in short measures life may perfect be.
BEN JONSON.

---

For every evil under the sun
There's a remedy, or there's none;
If there is one, try and find it —
If there isn't, never mind it.

---

Do not let us lie at all. Do not think of one falsity as harmless, and another as slight, and another as unintended. Cast them all aside: they may be light and accidental, but they are ugly soot from the smoke of the pit, for all that: and it is better that our hearts should be swept clean of them, without one care as to which is largest or blackest.
RUSKIN.

---

What is it to be a gentleman? It is to be honest, to be gentle, to be generous, to be brave, to be wise, and, possessing all these qualities, to exercise them in the most graceful outward manner.
THACKERAY.

## EACH AND ALL.

ALL are needed by each one;
Nothing is fair or good alone.
I thought the sparrow's note from heaven,
Singing at dawn on the alder bough.
I brought him home in his nest at even;
He sings the song; but it pleases not now;
For I did not bring home the river and sky:
He sang to my ear; they sang to my eye.
The delicate shells lay on the shore;
The bubbles of the latest wave
Fresh pearls to their enamel gave;
And the bellowing of the savage sea
Greeted their safe escape to me.
I wiped away the weeds and foam;
I fetched my sea-born treasures home;
But the poor, unsightly noisome things
Had left their beauty on the shore,
With the sun and the sand and the wild uproar.
EMERSON.

THE bravest trophy ever man obtained
Is that which o'er himself, himself hath gained.
POPE.

READING without purpose is sauntering, not exercise. More is got from one book on which the thought settles for definite end in knowledge, than from libraries skimmed over by a wandering eye. A cottage flower gives honey to the bee, a king's garden none to the butterfly.
EDWARD BULWER.

## VALUE OF PAIN.

HEARTS, like apples, are hard and sour,
Till crushed by pain's resistless power;
And yield their juices, rich and bland,
To none but sorrow's heavy hand.
The purest streams of human love
    Flow naturally never,
But gush by pressure from above.
J. G. HOLLAND.

THUS all must work with head or hand,
For self or others, good or ill;
Life is ordained to bear, like land,
Some fruit, be fallow as it will;
Evil has force itself to sow
Where we deny the healthy seed, —
And all our choice is this, — to grow
Pasture and grain, or noisome weed.
LORD HOUGHTON.

FLOWER, in the crannied wall,
    I pluck you out of the crannies;
Hold you here, root and all, in my hand.
Little flower, if I could understand
What you are, root and all, and all in all,
    I should know what God and man is.
TENNYSON.

READ not to contradict and confute; nor to believe and take for granted; nor to find talk and discourse: but to weigh and consider.
BACON.

## APOSTROPHE TO THE OCEAN.

Roll on, thou deep and dark blue Ocean, roll!
Ten thousand fleets sweep o'er thee in vain;
Man marks the earth with ruin — his control
Stops with the shore; upon the watery plain
The wrecks are all thy deeds, nor doth remain
A shadow of man's ravage, save his own,
When in a moment, like a drop of rain,
He sinks into thy depths with bubbling groan,
Without a grave, unknell'd, uncoffin'd, and unknown.
Byron.

Thanks to the human heart by which we live,
Thanks to its tenderness, its joys and fears;
To me the meanest flower that blows can give
Thoughts that do often lie too deep for tears.
Wordsworth.

But pleasures are like poppies spread;
You seize the flower, its bloom is shed;
Or, like the snow-fall in the river,
A moment white, then melts forever.
Robert Burns.

Conscience distasteful truths may tell,
But mark her sacred lessons well;
With her, whoever lives at strife,
Loses his better friend for life.

A man can do what he ought to do; and when he says he cannot he will not. Fichte.

## A MOTHER'S LOVE.

A MOTHER'S love — how sweet the name!
    What is a mother's love?
A noble, pure, and tender flame,
    Enkindled from above,
To bless a heart of earthly mould;
The warmest love that can grow cold;
    This is a mother's love.
                  JAMES MONTGOMERY.

WHOEVER fights, whoever falls,
Justice conquers evermore,
Justice after as before, —
And he who battles on her side,
God, though he were ten times slain,
Crowns him victor glorified, —
Victor over death and pain,
Forever.                              EMERSON.

EVERY wise observer knows,
    Every watchful gazer sees;
Nothing grand or beautiful grows,
    Save by gradual, slow degrees;
Ye who toil with a purpose high,
    And fondly the proud result await,
Murmur not, as the hours go by,
    That the season is long, the harvest is late.

    Sow good services; sweet remembrances will spring from them.                  MME. DE STAEL.

## THREE WORDS OF STRENGTH.

THERE are three lessons I would write,
  Three words, as with a burning pen,
In tracings of eternal light,
  Upon the hearts of men.

Have Hope. Though clouds environ round,
  And gladness hides her face in scorn,
Put off the shadow from thy brow:
  No night but hath its morn.

Have Faith. Where'er thy bark is driven,—
  The calm's disport, the tempest's mirth,—
Know this: God rules the hosts of heaven,
  The inhabitants of earth.

Have Love. Not love alone for one,
  But man, as man, thy brother call;
And scatter, like a circling sun,
  Thy charities on all.
                                    SCHILLER.

---

WERE I so tall to reach the pole,
  Or grasp the ocean in my span,
I must be measured by my soul:
  The mind's the standard of the man.

---

YOUNG men who spend many years at school and college are too apt to forget the great end of life, which is to be and to do, not to read and brood over what other men have been and done.         WILLIAM MATHEWS.

## KNOWLEDGE AND WISDOM.

Who loves not Knowledge? Who shall rail
    Against her beauty? May she mix
    With men and prosper! Who shall fix
Her pillars? Let her work prevail.

But on her forehead sits a fire:
    She sets her forward countenance
    And leaps into the future chance,
Submitting all things to desire.

Half grown as yet, a child, and vain,
    She cannot fight the fear of death.
    What is she, cut from love and faith,
But some wild Pallas from the brain

Of Demons? Fiery-hot to burst
    All barriers in her onward race
    For power. Let her know her place;
She is the second, not the first.

A higher hand must make her mild,
    If all be not in vain; and guide
    Her footsteps, moving side by side
With Wisdom, like the younger child.
                  TENNYSON, "*In Memoriam.*"

---

    Let your truth stand sure,
        And the world is true;
    Let your heart keep pure —
        And the world will, too.
                  GEORGE HOUGHTON.

## THE INFLUENCE OF NATURE.

NATURE never did betray
The heart that loved her; 'tis her privilege
Through all the years of this our life, to lead
From joy to joy: for she can so inform
The mind that is within us, so impress
With quietness and beauty, and so feed
With lofty thoughts, that neither evil tongues,
Rash judgments, nor the sneers of selfish men,
Nor greetings where no kindness is, nor all
The dreary intercourse of daily life,
Shall e'er prevail against us, or disturb
Our cheerful faith that all which we behold
Is full of blessings.
WORDSWORTH.

---

THE curtain of the dark
  Is pierced by many a rent;
Out of the star-wells, spark on spark
  Trickles through night's torn tent.

Grief is a tattered tent
  Wherethrough God's light doth shine.
Who glances up at every rent
  Shall catch a ray divine.
LUCY LARCOM.

---

I WOULD not waste my spring of youth
In idle dalliance: I would plant rich seeds,
To blossom in my manhood, and bear fruit when I am
  old.
HILLHOUSE.

## PRAYER.

MORE things are wrought by prayer
Than this world dreams of. Wherefore, let thy voice
Rise like a fountain for me night and day.
For what are men better than sheep or goats
That nourish a blind life within the brain,
If, knowing God, they lift not hands of prayer
Both for themselves and those that call them friend?
For so the whole round earth is every way
Bound by gold chains about the feet of God.
TENNYSON.

LIVE while you live, the epicure would say,
And seize the pleasures of the present day;
Live while you live, the sacred preacher cries,
And give to God each moment as it flies.
Lord, in my views let both united be;
I live in pleasure when I live to thee.
PHILIP DODDRIDGE.

### WEARINESS
Can snore upon the flint, when restive Sloth
Finds the down pillow hard.
SHAKESPEARE, "*Cymbeline.*"

TEACH me to feel another's woe,
  To hide the fault I see;
That mercy I to others show,
  That mercy show to me.
ALEXANDER POPE.

## GREAT THOUGHTS.

Who can mistake great thoughts?
They seize upon the mind; arrest, and search,
And shake it; bow the tall soul as by wind;
Rush over it like rivers over reeds,
Which quaver in the current; turn us cold,
And pale, and voiceless; leaving in the brain
A rocking and a ringing, — glorious,
But momentary; madness might it last,
And close the soul with Heaven as with a seal.
PHILIP JAMES BAILEY, "Festus."

---

Where lies the land to which the ship would go?
Far, far ahead, is all her seamen know.
And where the land she travels from? Away,
Far, far behind, is all that they can say.
ARTHUR HUGH CLOUGH.

---

But whether on the scaffold high,
   Or in the battle's van,
The fittest place where man can die
   Is where he dies for man!
MICHAEL J. BARRY.

---

He who has a thousand friends,
   Has not a friend to spare;
But he who has one enemy,
   Will meet him everywhere.
RALPH WALDO EMERSON.

## THE STRONG WILL.

O WELL for him whose will is strong!
He suffers, but he will not suffer long;
He suffers, but he cannot suffer wrong:
For him nor moves the loud world's random mock,
Nor all Calamity's hugest waves confound,
Who seems a promontory of rock,
That compass'd round with turbulent sound,
In middle ocean meets the surging shock,
Tempest buffeted, citadel crown'd.
TENNYSON.

THEY only the victory win
Who have fought the good fight, and have vanquished
    the demon that tempts us within;
Who have held to their faith unseduced by the prize
    that the world holds on high;
Who have dared for a high cause to suffer, resist, fight,
    — if need be, to die.
W. W. STORY.

THEY are slaves who dare not choose
Wrong and hatred and abuse,
Rather than in silence shrink
From the truth they need must think;
They are slaves who dare not be
In the right with two or three.
JAMES RUSSELL LOWELL.

NEVER contract a friendship with a man that is not better than thyself.
CONFUCIUS.

## THE STARS.

YE stars! which are the poetry of heaven!
If in your bright leaves we would read the fate
Of men and empires, — 'tis to be forgiven,
That in our aspirations to be great,
Our destinies o'erleap their mortal state,
And claim a kindred with you; for ye are
A beauty and a mystery, and create
In us such love and reverence from afar,
That fortune, fame, power, life, have named them-
    selves a star.
BYRON.

## TRUTH.

IT fortifies my soul to know
That though I perish, truth is so,
That howsoe'er I stray and range,
Whate'er I do, thou dost not change.
I steadier step when I recall
That, if I slip, thou dost not fall.
ARTHUR HUGH CLOUGH.

ALL is of God! if He but wave His hand,
    The mists collect, the rain falls thick and loud,
Till, with a smile of light on sea and land,
    Lo! He looks back from the departing cloud.

Angels of life and death alike are His;
    Without His leave they pass no threshold o'er;
Who, then, would wish or dare, believing this,
    Against His messengers to shut the door?
LONGFELLOW.

## MEMORY.

HAIL, memory, hail! in thy exhaustless mine
From age to age unnumbered treasures shine!
Thought and her shadowy brood thy call obey,
And Place and Time are subject to thy sway!
Thy pleasures most we feel, when most alone;
The only pleasures we can call our own.
Lighter than air, Hope's summer-visions die,
If but a fleeting cloud obscure the sky;
If but a beam of sober Reason play,
So Fancy's fairy frost-work melts away!
But can the wiles of Art, the grasp of Power,
Snatch the rich relics of a well-spent hour?
These, when the trembling spirit wings her flight,
Pour round her path a stream of living light,
And gild those pure and perfect realms of rest
Where Virtue triumphs and her sons are blest!

SAMUEL ROGERS.

## MUSIC OF THE SPHERES.

LOOK, how the floor of heaven
Is thick inlaid with patines of bright gold;
There's not the smallest orb, which thou beholdest,
But in his motion like an angel sings,
Still quiring to the young-eyed cherubins:
Such harmony is in immortal souls;
But whilst this muddy vesture of decay
Doth grossly close it in, we cannot hear it.

SHAKESPEARE, "*Merchant of Venice.*"

## FAME AND DUTY.

"What shall I do, lest life in silence pass?"
    "And if it do,
And never prompt the bray of noisy brass,
    What need'st thou rue?
Remember, age to ocean deeps are mate;
    The shallows roar:
Worth to the ocean, — fame is but the bruit
    Along the shore."

"What shall I do to be forever known?"
    "Thy duty ever."
"This did full many who yet slept unknown."
    "Oh, never, never!
Think'st thou perchance that they remain unknown
    Whom thou know'st not?
By angel trumps in heaven, their praise is blown —
    Divine their lot."

"What shall I do to gain eternal life?"
    "Discharge aright
The simple dues with which each day is rife,
    Yea, with thy might.
Ere perfect scheme of action thou devise,
    Will life be fled,
Where he, whoever acts as conscience cries,
    Shall live, though dead."
SCHILLER.

Who does the best his circumstances allow,
Does well, acts nobly; angels could no more.
YOUNG.

## MILTON ON HIS BLINDNESS.

When I consider how my light is spent
   Ere half my days, in this dark world and wide,
   And that one talent which is death to hide,
Lodged with me useless, though my soul more bent
To serve therewith my Maker, and present
   My true account, lest He, returning, chide;
   "Doth God exact day-labor light denied?"
I fondly ask; but patience, to prevent
That murmur, soon replies, "God doth not need
   Either man's work, or his own gifts; who best
   Bear His mild yoke, they serve Him best. His state
Is kingly; thousands at his bidding speed,
   And post o'er land and ocean without rest;
   They also serve who only stand and wait.

## SMALL THINGS.

'Tis a little thing
To give a cup of water; yet its draught
Of cool refreshment, drained by fevered lips,
May give a thrill of pleasure to the frame
More exquisite than when nectarean juice
Renews the life of joy in happier hours.
It is a little thing to speak a phrase
Of common comfort, which, by daily use,
Has almost lost its sense; yet on the ear
Of him who thought to die unmourned, 'twill fall
Like choicest music.
                             Talfourd.

## ABUSE OF AUTHORITY.

O, IT is excellent
To have a giant's strength; but it is tyrannous
To use it like a giant. Could great men thunder
As Jove himself does, Jove would ne'er be quiet;
For every pelting, petty officer
Would use his heaven for thunder; nothing but thunder.
Merciful heaven!
Thou rather, with thy sharp and sulphurous bolt,
Split'st the unwedgeable and gnarled oak,
Than the soft myrtle. — O, but man, proud man!
Drest in a little brief authority,
Most ignorant of what he's most assured,
His glassy essence, — like an angry ape,
Plays such fantastic tricks before high heaven,
As make the angels weep: who, with our spleens,
Would all themselves laugh mortal.

SHAKESPEARE, "Measure for Measure."

---

So live, that when thy summons comes to join
The innumerable caravan that moves
To the pale realms of shade, where each shall take
His chamber in the silent halls of death,
Thou go not, like the quarry-slave at night,
Scourged to his dungeon; but, sustained and soothed
By an unfaltering trust, approach thy grave
Like one who wraps the drapery of his couch
About him, and lies down to pleasant dreams.

BRYANT.

## MUTUAL FORGIVENESS.

No ceremony that to great ones 'longs,
Not the king's crown, nor the deputed sword,
The marshal's truncheon, nor the judge's robe,
Become them with one-half so good a grace
As mercy does.
Why, all the souls that were, were forfeit once,
And He that might the vantage best have took,
Found out the remedy. How would you be,
If He, which is the top of judgment, should
But judge you as you are? O, think on that;
And mercy then will breathe within your lips,
Like man new made.
SHAKESPEARE, "*Measure for Measure.*"

---

IF solid happiness we prize,
Within our breast this jewel lies;
   And they are fools who roam;
The world has nothing to bestow;
From our own selves our joys must flow,
   And that dear hut, — our home.
NATHANIEL COTTON.

---

THE heights by great men reached and kept
   Were not attained by sudden flight,
But they, while their companions slept,
   Were toiling upward through the night.
LONGFELLOW.

## THE CHOIR INVISIBLE.

O, MAY I join the choir invisible
Of those immortal dead who live again
In minds made better by their presence; live
In pulses stirred to generosity,
In deeds of daring rectitude, in scorn
Of miserable aims that end with self,
In thoughts sublime that pierce the night like stars,
And with their mild persistence urge men's minds
To vaster issues.
   May I reach
That purest heaven, — be to other souls
The cup of strength in some great agony,
Enkindle generous ardor, feed pure love,
Beget the smiles that have no cruelty,
Be the sweet presence of good diffused,
And in diffusion ever more intense!
So shall I join the choir invisible,
Whose music is the gladness of the world.
    GEORGE ELIOT (Mrs. George H. Lewes).

---

HAPPY he whom neither wealth nor fashion,
Nor the march of the encroaching city,
  Drives an exile
From the heart of his ancestral homestead.

We may build more splendid habitations,
Fill our rooms with paintings and with sculptures,
  But we cannot
Buy with gold the old associations!
    LONGFELLOW.

## HOME.

But where to find that happiest spot below,
Who can direct, when all pretend to know?
The shuddering tenant of the frigid zone
Boldly proclaims that happiest spot his own;
Extols the treasures of his stormy seas,
And his long nights of revelry and ease:
The naked negro, panting at the line,
Boasts of his golden sands and palmy wine,
Basks in the glare, or stems the tepid wave,
And thanks his gods for all the good they gave.
Such is the patriot's boast, where'er we roam,
His first, best country is at home.
— Oliver Goldsmith.

## LOVE OF COUNTRY.

Breathes there a man with soul so dead,
Who never to himself hath said,
   This is my own, my native land?
Whose heart has ne'er within him burned
As home his footsteps he hath turned,
   From wandering on a foreign strand?
If such there breathe, go, mark him well;
For him no minstrel raptures swell!
High though his titles, proud his name,
Boundless his wealth as wish can claim:
Despite those titles, power, and pelf,
The wretch, concentered all in self,
Living, shall forfeit fair renown,
And, doubly dying, shall go down
To the vile dust from whence he sprung,
Unwept, unhonored, and unsung. — Sir Walter Scott.

## THE DECLARATION OF INDEPENDENCE.

WHEN, in the course of human events, it becomes necessary for one people to dissolve the political bands which have connected them with another, and to assume, among the powers of the earth, the separate and equal station to which the laws of Nature and of Nature's God entitle them, a decent respect to the opinions of mankind requires that they should declare the causes which impel them to the separation.

We hold these truths to be self-evident: that all men are created equal; that they are endowed by their Creator with certain unalienable rights; that among these are life, liberty, and the pursuit of happiness. That, to secure these rights, governments are instituted among men, deriving their just powers from the consent of the governed; that, whenever any form of government becomes destructive of these ends, it is the right of the people to alter or to abolish it, and to institute a new government, laying its foundations on such principles, and organizing its powers in such form, as to them shall seem most likely to effect their safety and happiness.

. . . . . . . .

We, therefore, the representatives of the United States of America, in general Congress assembled, appealing to the Supreme Judge of the world for the rectitude of our intentions, do, in the name and by the authority of the good people of these colonies, solemnly publish and declare, that these united colonies are, and of right ought to be, free and independent States; that they are absolved from all allegiance to the British crown, and that all political connection between them and the State of Great Britain is, and ought to be, totally dissolved; and that, as free and independent States, they have full power to levy war, conclude peace, contract alliances, establish commerce, and to do all other acts and things which independent States may of right do. And, for the support of this declaration, with a firm reliance on the protection of Divine Providence, we mutually pledge to each other, our lives, our fortunes, and our sacred honor.

THOMAS JEFFERSON.

THE poorest man may in his cottage bid defiance to all the force of the crown. It may be frail; its roof may shake; the wind may blow through it; the storms may enter, the rain may enter, — but the King of England cannot enter! All his forces dare not cross the threshold of the ruined tenement.

WILLIAM PITT, Earl of Chatham.

# CLASSICS FOR CHILDREN.

IT is proposed to publish from standard authors a number of works, as nearly complete as possible, adapting them to children between the ages of nine and fifteen, in our Grammar Schools. They will be printed in large type, on good paper, and substantially bound, and sold at a very low price. (*The above is a specimen of the type to be used in these books.*)
The following two volumes are now ready: —

### ROBINSON CRUSOE,

The famous English Classic. Edited, for Supplementary Reading in Schools, by W. H. LAMBERT, Supt. of Schools, Malden, Mass. Bound in boards, 263 pages. Introduction price, 30 cents.

The original work has been abridged by omitting a few of the more uninteresting episodes, and by condensing many of the lengthy moral reflections, where they seem to impede the onward flow of the story. All the gross terms and allusions, which render the complete text unfit for schools, have been removed; and the long and involved sentences, which characterize the writers of the age of Defoe, have been cast into simple form, while the diction of the author has been carefully preserved. The story has been divided into chapters, and judicious notes have been added, sufficient to explain the text.

### SHAKESPEARE'S MERCHANT OF VENICE.

HUDSON and LAMB. Bound in boards. Life, 10 pages; Lamb's story, 16 pages; Text and Notes, 81 pages; or 107 pages in all. Introduction price, 20 cents.

It contains Hudson's Life of Shakespeare, and about two-thirds of the Text and Notes of his School Edition. Nothing is omitted that would impair the value of the work for children; but, on the contrary, by introducing them directly to the leading characters, their interest in it is heightened.

The story of the play is taken directly from Charles and Mary Lamb's "Tales from Shakespeare."

# Geographies and Globes.

### Our World, No. I.; or, First Lessons in Geography.

By MARY L. HALL. Small quarto. 119 pages. Mailing Price, 65 cts.; Introduction, 50 cts.; Exchange, 35 cts.

### Our World, No. II.; or, Second Series of Lessons

in *Geography*. By MARY L. HALL. With fine illustrations of the various countries, the inhabitants and their occupations, and two distinct series of Maps; 5 pages physical, and 19 pages political, of finely engraved copper-plates. Quarto. 176 pages. Mailing Price, $1.65; Introduction, $1.20; Exchange, 75 cents.

Designed to give clear and lasting impressions of the different countries and inhabitants of the earth, rather than to tax the memory with mere names and details. They are the result of the best professional skill, embody the true spirit of geographical reform, and teach *ideas* rather than *words*. They are the only books not having ready-made answers, and the only books combining the political, physical, and historical geography of a country in the same lesson. The text is so connected as to serve admirably as a reading-book.

**It has been used in the cities of Newton and Cambridge, Mass., almost since the date of its publication (ten years since), and is still used in these cities.**

E. **Hunt,** *recently Supt. of Schools, Newton, Mass.:* They have been in use here ten years, and have continued to grow in popularity. It is made a very interesting reading-book the fourth year of school, studied and recited the fifth, and geography is completed the sixth and seventh years.

F. **Cogswell,** *Supt. of Schools, Cambridge:* Our World, No. I., has been used in this city for a series of years, and I have no doubt that it is more highly valued as a text-book at the present time than during the first years after its introduction.

## The Fitz Globe.

Clearly illustrates all the Phenomena produced by the Sun's Relations to the Earth, and is the First Globe to illustrate the Sun's Daily Course, or indicate the Interval of Twilight, or represent one's Horizon, without falsifying the existing relation of the Earth's Axis to its Orbit.

Six-inch Globe (Retail Price) . . . . . . . . . . . . . . . $15.00
Twelve-inch Globe (Retail Price) . . . . . . . . . . . . 30.00
(*No charge for packing.*)

A new Map has just been executed for the Fitz Globe by a very skilful engraver, and it is now "the latest and best engraved Globe either in England or the United States."

Most of the globes now for sale in this country were engraved over twenty-five years ago, and have only a few popular discoveries added to the old plates. Our new Map represents recent discoveries, and is based on the latest and best authorities.

In the Arctic Regions the results of the most recent expeditions will be found carefully detailed. Europe exhibits the latest political divisions, with special reference to France, the new German Empire, and Italy. In Asia, the extension of Russian power is indicated by important changes on the former limits of Turkestan; while the new frontiers of Persia, Afghanistan, and Beloochistan have been carefully indicated. India, China, and Japan have also been presented in their most modern aspect.

In Central Africa the results of the researches of Livingstone, Stanley, Cameron, and other distinguished explorers are represented. In North America the new States are shown with their latest changes of boundaries, while all new towns of importance are

England.
Scotland.
Ireland.
British Isles.
Canada, Nova Scotia, etc.
United States.
South America.
France.
Spain and Portugal.
Italy.
Central Europe.

Orkney and Shetland.
Asia.
India.
Africa.
Cape Colony.
America.
North America.
Australia.
New Zealand (in Counties).
Pacific Ocean.

CLASSICAL AND SCRIPTURAL GEOGRAPHY.

Cæsar de Bello Gallico.
Orbis Veteribus Notus.
Italia Antiqua.
Græcia Antiqua.
Asia Minor.
Orbis Romanus.

Travels of St. Paul.
Outline Map of Countries bordering on Mediterranean.
Canaan and Palestine.
Bible Countries.

See page 91 for description of Ginn & Heath's Classical Atlas.

PHYSICAL GEOGRAPHY.

World, in Hemispheres.
Europe.
Asia.

Africa.
America.

## Johnston's Small Wall Maps.

Size, 33 × 27 inches. Colored, and Mounted on Cloth and Rollers. Price, $3.00 each; Introduction, $2.40 each.

Eastern and Western Hemispheres (one Map).
World, Mercator's Projection.
Eastern Hemisphere.
Western Hemisphere.
Europe.
England.
Scotland.
Ireland.
British Isles.
Asia.
Canaan and Palestine.
Africa.

America.
North America.
Canada, United States, and Mexico.
South America.
St. Paul's Travels.
A Map illustrative of Geographical Terms (with Glossary).
Chronological Chart of Ancient History (with Glossary).
Chart of the Metric System of Weights and Measures.

# English Grammar.

## *Elementary Lessons in English. Part First:*
"*HOW TO SPEAK AND WRITE CORRECTLY.*" By W. D. WHITNEY of Yale College, and Mrs. N. L. KNOX. 12mo. Cloth. 192 pages. Mailing price, 50 cts.; Introduction, 30 cts.; Exchange, 22 cts.

This Part contains *no technical grammar*. It is designed to give children such a knowledge of the English Language as will enable them to *speak*, *write*, and *use* it with accuracy and force. It is made up of exercises to increase and improve the vocabulary, lessons in enunciation, pronunciation, spelling, sentence-making, punctuation; the use of capitals, abbreviations, drill in writing number-forms, gender-forms, and the possessive-form, letter-writing, and such other matters pertaining to the art of the language as may be taught simply, clearly, and profitably. Many and varied oral and written exercises supplement every lesson.

## *The Teacher's Edition of Elementary Lessons*
*in English.* To accompany PART I.: "*HOW TO SPEAK AND WRITE CORRECTLY.*" Prepared by Mrs. N. L. KNOX. 12mo. Cloth. 323 pages. Mailing price, 80 cts.; Introduction price, 60 cts.

The "Teacher's Edition" contains the entire text of the children's book, and, in addition, plans for developing the lessons of the text, observation lessons, dictation and test exercises, questions for oral and written reviews, materials for composition exercises, plans for conducting picture lessons, a story lesson, etc., etc., etc.

In a preliminary chapter (*The Teacher's Guide*) will be found a discussion of the Pestalozzian principles of education and instruction, of the art of questioning and the laws of questioning, of methods of correcting oral and written mistakes, and of oral lessons — how to prepare them, and how to give them. This includes also material and plans for Oral Lessons in Language for the first, second, third, and fourth years in school. There is no book published in this country which is so clear, direct, and complete a manual for the use of teachers.

## Elementary Lessons in English. Part Second:

"*HOW TO TELL THE PARTS OF SPEECH.*" By W. D. WHITNEY of Yale College, and Mrs. N. L. KNOX. [*In preparation.*]

For description of Part I., see page 37.

The pupil no longer studies words with reference merely to their. meaning, pronunciation, spelling, written form, and use to express ideas, but as elements of sentences, — as *Parts of Speech*, — and considers each with reference to its use in the sentence. The technical terms of grammar are employed, and the more obvious rules of syntax are taught.

The vocabulary lessons and exercises for practice in oral and written composition are novel and valuable. Rules for spelling, for the use of capitals, marks of punctuation, and marks used by proof-readers, are added as occasion requires. A *resumé* of these, a table of synonymes, a table giving the sounds and diacritical marks of the consonants, and an additional list of abbreviations, make up the Appendix.

The *Method* of the book rests not upon theory, or experiment merely, but upon successful practice.

## Whitney's Essentials of English Grammar.

For the Use of High Schools, Academies, and the Upper Grades of Grammar Schools. By Professor W. D. WHITNEY of Yale College. 12mo. Cloth. 260 pages. Mailing price, $1.00; Introduction, 70 cts.; Exchange, 40 cts.

This is an *English* Grammar of the English Language, prepared by the best philologist in the country. It is clear, practical, and complete. It proceeds from facts to principles, and from these to classifications and definitions. Mechanical forms, unnecessary classifications, and abstract definitions are avoided.

The exercises, selected from the best English writers, leave none of the usual and regular forms of English structure untouched.

The plan of analysis is simple. The ordinary method of Gender in Nouns is displaced by one truer and far simpler. The sharp distinction of verb-phrases or compound forms from the real verb-forms is original and scholarly.

# Vocal Music.

## The National Music Course.

For Public Schools. By L. W. MASON, late Supervisor of Music in the Public Schools of Boston, now Director of Music in the Empire of Japan, and JULIUS EICHBERG, Director of Music in the schools of Boston, and J. B. SHARLAND, and H. E. HOLT, Supervisors of Music in the Public Schools of Boston, Mass.

FIRST MEDAL.     FIRST MEDAL.     FIRST MEDAL.

*Vienna, 1873.*     *Philadelphia, 1876.*     *Paris, 1878.*

☞ We send our **SPECIAL MUSIC CIRCULAR** on application. It contains interesting extracts on the "*Influence of Vocal Music*"; answers through numerous school officials and music teachers the question as to whether *Music should be taught in the public schools;* estimates the cost per pupil for its introduction; gives valuable information to teachers as to best methods; and contains the programmes used in several cities.

This course includes the following books and charts: —

## First Music Reader.

By LUTHER WHITING MASON, for fifteen years Supervisor of Music in the Primary Schools of Boston. 16mo. 96 pages. Mailing Price, 20 cents; Introduction, 15 cents; Exchange, 10 cents.

To the author's fitness for the work Supt. Philbrick bears the following testimony: —

A teacher of large experience, an enthusiast in the work, a man of the rarest genius for teaching children, a student of pedagogy, with a spirit of self-sacrifice that constantly reminded me of the career of Pestalozzi, thoroughly acquainted with the best things that had been thought and said and done about teaching children vocal music.

Larkin Dunton, Prin. of the Boston Normal School, says: —

I have had better opportunities, perhaps, than any other man to know Mr. Mason's methods of teaching, because he has been more intimately connected with me in his work. He had charge of the music in the primary schools under my immediate care four or five years, and then taught methods in music as much longer in the Boston Normal School under my charge. And now I wish to say that I have never known the philosophy of methods of instruction better illustrated, either in music, or in any other subject, than it has been in the lessons that I have heard him give To many of these lessons I have listened for the fourth or fifth time, and have enjoyed them highly as works of art, so perfectly were they planned, so skilfully were they executed.

The songs in this little book are admirably adapted to rote singing. A part of the songs can then be sung over by note, the former rote singing helping to fix the intervals in the mind, and strengthening the association between the notes and tones. It should be taken as an accompaniment to the **First Series of Charts**, containing as it does a partial reprint of the lessons of the Charts, with different illustrations, review of the Keys, exercises to be written, and intonation exercises.

A knowledge of the scale, staff, cleff, and the simple varieties of measure are taught, as well as the ordinary dynamic marks; and the transposition into nine keys is given, as well as practice in the various keys. The compass of music in the Exercises and Songs is such as to peculiarly assist in the proper vocal training of young children.

The **First Reader** and the **First Series of Charts** are intended for children from five to eight years of age.

The **Teachers' Manual**, described on page 179, gives all necessary instruction to teachers using this book or the **First Chart**.

*See page 182 for opinions of those using the book.*

## Second Music Reader.

By LUTHER WHITING MASON. 16mo. 96 pages. Mailing Price, 22 cents; Introduction, 16 cents; Exchange, 12 cents.

Prepared to accompany the **Second Series of Charts**, the exercises and songs illustrating the principles treated of in the Charts.

Before commencing the **Second Series of Readers and Charts**, the pupils are supposed to have gone through the **First Series** or their equivalent in some other course. It is also supposed that the ear and voice have been trained so that the pupils are able to sing several songs tastefully by rote; and the sense of rhythm has been somewhat developed. They should be familiar with some of the characters used in musical notation, and should name them at sight, such as staff, G-clef; whole, half, quarter, and eighth notes, and their corresponding rests; measures, bars, and the double-bar. They will have become familiar with these while learning their exercises and songs.

All through the primary course the *ear* should lead; but when pupils enter the grammar schools, at about the age of eight or nine years, and commence the **Second Series of Music Charts** and the **Second Music Reader**, the manner of proceeding should be changed to a great extent. The *eye* should then lead, and music be made more of an intellectual study.

Only the major scale in nine keys is used in this book. It takes up the elements in more rapid progression, introducing more difficult varieties of measure, two-part harmonies, and a review of the keys. Pupils, not too young, can take up the **Second Reader** and the **Second Series of Charts**, even if they have not been through the **First**; while those who have will find new exercises and advanced lessons to interest and carry them gradually forward.

The **Teachers' Manual**, described on page 179, gives a course of lessons preparatory to taking up the **Second** and **Third Series of Charts** by those who have not been through the **First Series**, and as an aid to teachers who know but little about music.

*See page 182 for opinions of Music Teachers.*

## Third Music Reader.

By LUTHER WHITING MASON. 16mo. 96 pages. Mailing Price, 22 cents; Introduction, 16 cents; Exchange, 12 cents.

The **Third Reader** is designed to be used in connection with the **Third Series of Charts**, and has its songs based on the triads and chords taught in the Charts, and enables teachers to carry out practically what the pupil has learned theoretically from the Chart. Before commencing this course, the pupils are supposed to have gone through the **Second Series of Music Charts** and **Second Music Reader**, and to be able to sing easy songs, in two parts, in nine different keys of the major scale.

They are now to continue the two-part singing, but are to be led to recognize the harmonic relation of sounds, as derived from the

*MUSIC.*

triads of the major and minor scales, and the chords of the seventh and ninth. Two, three, and even four parts are attempted, but only in such chords as can be taken by girls, and boys before their voices have changed. It takes up the various intervals, major and minor thirds, triads, and the most usual forms of the chords of the seventh and ninth.

*See page 182 for commendations of the Course.*

## Intermediate Music Reader.

By LUTHER WHITING MASON. 16mo. 192 pages. Mailing Price, 45 cents; Introduction, 30 cents; Exchange, 20 cents.

Contains the **Second** and **Third Music Readers** in one volume.

## Fourth Music Reader.

By JULIUS EICHBERG and J. B. SHARLAND. 8vo. 336 pages. Mailing Price, $1.05; Introduction, 75 cents; Exchange, 50 cents.

The **Fourth Reader** and the **Fourth Series of Charts** give special attention to expression. The pupil, in commencing the **Fourth Reader**, is expected to have some ability in reading music; and this work, as the name implies, is a continuation of previous instruction. But every teacher of experience well knows the value of reviewing former studies; and at this stage of progress in musical education it is well to examine carefully all previous work. To this end the theory or grammar of music is introduced.

This book contains, therefore, a complete system of musical instruction. The music introduced is of a high order, and by the best masters, and is calculated to cultivate the taste, as well as to extend the knowledge and skill of the pupils.

This **Reader**, under a competent instructor, may be used in advanced grammar schools where no previous systematic instruction has been given. To this end, the first fifty pages of the book are devoted to a brief but thorough elementary course, with musical theory, original solfeggios, a complete system of triad practice, and sacred music and song, with accompaniment for the piano.

*See page 182 for commendations of the Course.*

## Abridged Fourth Music Reader.

8vo. 288 pages. Mailing Price, 85 cents; Introduction, 60 cents; Exchange, 40 cents.

Omits the first fifty pages of the above book which relate to "The Theory of Music."
The pupil is supposed to have mastered the tasks contained in the preceding books of the series; and the regular teachers, with the aid of the blackboard and the charts, ought to be able to make such explanations and give such instruction as the peculiar circumstances of the class may require.

## High School Music Reader for Mixed Voices.

By JULIUS EICHBERG, Director of Music in the Boston Public Schools. 8vo. 324 pages. Mailing Price, $1.05; Introduction, 75 cents; Exchange, 50 cents.

Contains a full course of Advanced Solfeggios for one and two voices, and a carefully selected number of easy *Four*-Part Songs, taken from the works of the best composers.

This work has been especially compiled to meet the growing wants of our mixed and boys' high schools for a higher grade of music than is contained in works now used in such schools. A sufficient number of sacred songs are introduced to render this book admirably adapted to devotional exercises as well as to the distinctive purposes of musical instruction. The Choruses have been selected for their musical worth, and are well adapted to the development of a sound musical taste.

Some knowledge of singing and of reading at sight is indispensable, previous to taking up the **High School Reader.** All the Solfeggios have been used for years in the Boston High Schools, and will be found to contain a great variety of rhythmical and melodic forms. They may be transposed whenever it becomes necessary, although most of them can be sung by pupils of a very small compass of voice.

N.B. — The Tenor Part in many of the songs may be either omitted or sung by the altos (boys).

## Teachers' Manual for First Series of Charts and

*Readers.* ("NATIONAL MUSIC TEACHER.") By L. W. MASON. 8vo. 72 pages. Mailing Price, 45 cents; Introduction, 30 cents.

The precise work of the teacher and class is shown, each step being carefully explained. In fact, the basis of the book is a series of verbatim reports of actual lessons given to little children by the author. The words of both teacher and pupils are reported, so that the exercise is brought vividly to the mind of any intelligent instructor.

## Teachers' Manual for Second and Third Series

*of Charts and Readers.* By L. W. MASON and H. E. HOLT. 12mo. 98 pages. Mailing Price, 45 cents; Introduction, 30 cents.

This book gives a course of lessons, showing how to present the **Second and Third Series of Charts** to those who have not been through the **First Series**, and as an aid to teachers who know but little about music. It contains also appendices on "French Time-Names" and the "Management of the Voice."

## National Music Charts.

FOR THE USE OF SINGING CLASSES, SEMINARIES, CONSERVATORIES, SCHOOLS, AND FAMILIES. By LUTHER WHITING MASON. In Four Series. Forty Charts each, size 25 × 36 inches. Price for each Series, by express, $8.50; Introduction, $7.00; Easel, $1.00. Sample-leaf of Charts sent free to any address.

An invaluable aid to teachers of common schools in imparting a practical knowledge of Music, and teaching children to sing at sight. They can be used on any easel the teacher may have at hand as readily as upon the one we manufacture, or they can be hung upon the wall.

*These charts will be found to commend themselves in the following particulars:* —

1. The lessons are printed from a newly invented and *patented* type, forming a beautiful page, large and distinct enough to be seen by the whole class at once.

2. They save the time of teacher and scholar.

## MUSIC.

3. They are so systematically and progressively arranged that even inexperienced teachers can scarcely fail to be successful with them.

4. They embody the results of many years' experience of a *practical teacher of children.*

5. They answer equally well for adults, being truly scientific without being dull.

6. They have been *proved by use*, having been permanently adopted in the public schools of hundreds of our leading cities and towns.

7. They bring about the successful *reading of music* in place of the *parrot-like rote-singing* hitherto prevalent in schools.

8. They furnish a good set of model school-songs in the various keys.

9. They secure a good position of the body (so essential to health) while singing, as the pupils are obliged to look upward in reading from them, instead of bending over a book.

10. They accustom the smallest children to carry parts independently in singing harmony.

11. They are neat and compact, requiring no use of chalk or crayon, and occupying, for *forty charts*, no more space in the schoolroom than is required for a single one of the ordinary pasteboard tablets.

12. They are cheap and durable, serving successive classes a number of years.

13. The saving of time, which would otherwise be used in writing blackboard exercises, makes it a matter of economy to furnish schools with them.

## The First Series of Charts.

Intended for use in the primary schools, or for children from five to eight years of age. By an easy and systematic progress a knowledge of the scale, staff, cleff, and the simple varieties of measure are taught, as well as the ordinary dynamic marks; and in the last part of the series the transposition into nine keys is given, as well as practice in the various keys. The pupils should become familiar with rote singing before any effort is made to teach notation. The compass of music in these charts is such as to peculiarly assist in the proper vocal training of young children. (*See description of First Music Reader.*)

## The Second Series of Charts.

Adapted to pupils of eight years and upward. The elements are taken up in more rapid progression than in the First Series, introducing more difficult varieties of measure, two-part harmonies, and a review of the keys. Pupils not too young can take up this series even if they have not been through the First; while those who have will find new exercises and advanced lessons to interest and carry them gradually forward. (*See description of Second Music Reader.*)

## The Third Series of Charts.

Fitted for those who have been through the Second, and takes up the various intervals, major and minor thirds, triads, and the most usual forms of the chords of the seventh and ninth. Three-part songs in nine keys are introduced to illustrate the harmonies taught, and pupils are advanced in the science of music as far as is practicable until boys' voices begin to change. (*See description of Third Music Reader.*)

## The Fourth Series of Charts.

By L. W. MASON and J. B. SHARLAND.

In this Series special attention is given to expression and taste, without which the most strict time and perfect tone would fail to please the cultivated ear.

www.ingramcontent.com/pod-product-compliance
Lightning Source LLC
Chambersburg PA
CBHW031446160426
43195CB00010BB/875